Tough Plants

for

CALIFORNIA GARDENS

Low Care, No Care, Tried and True Winners

635.09794
RVS

Copyright © 2005 Felder Rushing

All rights reserved. No part of this book may be reproduced or transmitted in any form, or by any means, electronic or mechanical, including photocopying, recording, or by any information storage and retrieval system, without permission in writing from the publisher.

Published by Cool Springs Press, a Division of Thomas Nelson, Inc., P.O. Box 141000, Nashville, Tennessee 37214.

Catalog in publication data is available.
ISBN: 1-5918-6189-6

First printing 2006
Printed in the United States of America
10 9 8 7 6 5 4 3 2 1

Managing Editor: Jenny Andrews
Cover Design: Becky Brawner, Unlikely Suburban Design
Production Artist: S.E. Anderson

Visit the Thomas Nelson website at www.ThomasNelson.com and the Cool Springs Press website at www.coolspringspress.net.

Photo Credits

Unless otherwise noted, photography provided by Felder Rushing.

William Adams: 68 (bottom), 74 (top), 139 (top), 209
Liz Ball and Rick Ray: 21, 35 (bottom), 50 (bottom), 53 (top), 54 (top), 58 (top), 59, 67 (middle), 76 (bottom), 79 (bottom), 80 (top), 89 (top), 139 (bottom), 200 (bottom), 217 (top)
John Cretti: 131 (bottom)
Tom Eltzroth: 26 (top), 27, 28 (top), 31 (top), 32 (top), 33, 34, 35 (top), 37 (top), 39, 40 (top), 43, 50 (top), 51, 52 (bottom), 56 (bottom), 57, 61, 64 (middle), 66 (bottom), 68 (top), 74 (bottom), 75, 76 (top), 77 (bottom), 81 (top), 82 (top), 83 (bottom), 87, 89 (bottom), 93 (bottom), 94 (bottom), 104 (bottom), 105 (top), 107, 108 (top), 111 (bottom), 112 (top), 115 (bottom), 117, 121, 123 (top), 12 (top), 128 (bottom), 129 (top), 132 (top), 134, 137 (bottom), 138 (bottom), 140, 143, 147 (top), 149 (top), 152 (bottom), 155, 157 (top), 160, 161 (bottom), 162 (bottom), 163 (top), 164 (top), 166 (top), 167, 169 (bottom), 171 (top), 173 (top), 185 (middle), 193 (top), 196 (bottom), 198 (bottom), 201 (bottom), 203 (top), 205 (top), 206, 208 (top), 211, 215 (top), 216 (top), 218 (bottom), 220 (bottom), 221 (bottom), 229 (top)
Lorenzo Gunn: 109 (bottom), 166 (bottom)
Pam Harper: 110 (middle), 124, 133 (top)
Kristen Llamas: 128 (top)
Peter Loewer: 64 (top), 65 (bottom)
Charles Mann: 67 (bottom), 122 (top), 136 (top), 170
Judy Mielke: 204 (top)
Stephen Pategas: 135 (bottom)
Jerry Pavia: 28 (bottom), 29 (top), 30 (top), 32 (bottom), 36 (top), 38 (top), 40 (bottom), 52 (top), 64 (bottom), 66 (middle & top), 67 (top), 68 (middle), 85, 110 (top), 125, 126 (top), 130, 131 (top), 132 (bottom), 134 (bottom), 136 (bottom), 137 (top), 141 (bottom), 150 (top), 151 (top), 156, 158, 164 (bottom), 165, 167, 168 (bottom), 169 (top), 173, 175 (top), 182 (bottom), 184 (top), 186 (bottom), 197 (bottom), 198 (top), 203 (bottom), 218 (top), 219 (bottom), 222 (bottom), 223 (top), 228 (top)
Neil Soderstrom: 69 (bottom)

FEB 1 5 2008

Tough Plants
for
CALIFORNIA GARDENS
Low Care, No Care, Tried and True Winners

Felder Rushing

COOL SPRINGS PRESS
A Division of Thomas Nelson Publishers
Since 1798
www.thomasnelson.com

CARLSBAD
CITY LIBRARY
Carlsbad, CA
92011
DISCARD

Dedication:

To Master Gardeners, who in return for extensive training in home horticulture provided by the University of California Cooperative Extension program, have volunteered untold thousands of hours of "payback" time working with neighbors, communities, public gardens, and children. Throughout the state they have "taken to the street" the very best of gardening—sometimes so cheerfully it makes you want to scream!

Acknowledgements:

I'm really serious here—this book could not have been completed without the in-depth help of many like-minded California horticulturists, botanic garden curators, designers, and Master Gardeners. The following great gardeners touched this book in meaningful, often crucial ways, mostly by helping me scout gardens for tough plants, participating in marathon late-night yakfests, and suffering barrages of nit-picking e-mails:

Samantha McTighe, Bob Tanem, Bruce Asakawa, Sharon Lovejoy, Joanie Finch, Judy and Helen Wong, Joe Seals, Julian Duval (and his wife Leslie, who puts up with a lot of garden weirdos), Kathy Musial, Leslie Feathers, Lili Singer, Lucy Tolmach, Lucy Warren, Marcia Donahue, Marianne Lipanovich, Nan Sterman, Pat Hammer, Pat Welsh, Rosalind Creasy, Saxon Holt, Shila Clement, Sisso Doyle, Steve and Donna Brigham, Susi Torre-Bueno, Vincent Lazaneo, the helpful owners and staffs of Bueno Creek Gardens, Native Sons nursery and San Marcos Growers, and participants in late-night gardenweb.com forums.

Each of the above is outstanding and well known in their communities, whether botanic garden, horticulture, garden writing (newspaper, books, magazines, and radio), and Master Gardeners. All had a direct influence on the author with their time, expertise, and patience, often sharing their personal "garden variety" gardens. We spent half our time backing up for second looks while exploring back alleys in small rural towns, and in mobile home parks.

I especially want to honor the insights, guidance, flexibility, patience (most of the time), and good cheer of friend and long-suffering editor Jenny Andrews. She has earned a special crown in Heaven. Her Cool Springs Press bosses, Ramona Wilkes and Hank McBride, have been real trusting gems and supporters as well.

Many, many thanks to each and all!

Table of Contents

Foreword

In my many years of being in the horticulture industry, especially in the teaching end, I've found that the vast majority of gardeners believe that the real challenge in

gardening is to produce a beautiful garden with minimal care. However, the "true" gardener likes to push and is willing to make the needed adjustments, work, sacrifice, whatever, to grow some prized possession. And what on earth is wrong with that. If a gardener is so inclined, he or she is welcome to brag about having a perfect lawn, or growing the first *Tagetes lucida* or *Isoplexis canariensis* in the neighborhood. It works.

Yet only a very tiny percentage of people want the challenge of growing really unsuitable plants, which involves not just extra time on the gardener's part, but also includes heavy resource use. Besides, some plants are too specialized for the average gardener.

While we don't all need to grow cactus and succulents, it is a good idea to stay away from water guzzling plants, or those that need constant fertilizing or regular spraying.

Better yet, why not share one's failures as well? Could be that's the most important experience to pass on to others. For every jacaranda that someone is succeeding with in one part of the state, there are hundreds that limp along ungracefully, and thousands that are no longer around to prove that jacarandas don't like it here. Maybe the past owners need to put out a sign: "Jacaranda died here."

Everyone is welcome to dig, bag, chill, spit, and turn summersaults to get a temperamental posy to do just right. But telling others to do this is less than good advice. There is plenty of "fun" in gardening to keep *everyone* busy; we don't need "work" to make gardening fun.

In this book, Felder presents us with the "what-does-best" plants—the plants that fill our gardens with the least care needed, and that, in turn, allow us more quality time in our garden oases. For those who want a landscape of entirely low-maintenance, this is certainly the listing of the lowest.

"Tough," as in the title of this book, is Felder's word for "hearty." "Tough" is also the word for Felder's no-nonsense style that cuts through the—let us say—manure of the plant selection process.

Joe Seals is a landscape designer and horticulture consultant and teacher in Santa Maria.

Green
SIDE UP

This book is about nearly indestructible plants for California. Its aim is to increase the satisfaction of gardeners by highlighting what decades of experience have shown to be the toughest survivors across our country's third largest state.

Here you will find the kinds of plants that California garden experts agree to be beautiful, adaptable, useful, and downright easy to grow, with little or no care. That's the premise of this book—to recommend very hardy stuff that has been planted by a wide range of gardeners, of all styles and abilities, for many years, and that have proven themselves to grow well without a lot of "artificial life support."

Some of the plants are common as ants, even considered "weedy" in some gardens; others are cutting edge new varieties. All can be used very successfully in nearly any garden style, from suburban front yards to the finest botanical gardens.

Stuck in the Middle with You

In spite of regional bickering between horticulturists (which reminds me of the old Stealer's Wheels hit song, "Clowns to the left of me, jokers to the right, here I am—stuck in the middle with you"), California *gardeners* are pretty much alike.

Sure, many popular plants change dramatically from one area to another, especially in the heavily-populated areas of Southern California, San Francisco Bay area, and the Central Valley. Heck, they change from one side of town to the other, and the farther from the coast you are (every mile you go, the temperatures rise). But some universal truths have been uncovered about gardening in the Golden State. The challenges of climate and soil affect us all and we look for solutions with the same gusto. High-end tropical plant collectors in Santa Barbara have nothing over backyard daylily hybridizers in Fresno; miserable native soil and fog affect all equally.

Water shortages, onslaughts of invasive exotic plants, and the crushing development of new housing tracts are major ecological issues. Yet more direct concerns are every gardener's frustration over getting water to cherished garden plants on a regular basis, weeding the flower bed, and getting along with new neighbors from who-knows-where. This book attempts to deal with all these issues.

Scratching and Sniffing

Before wrapping up this book, I meandered over an astounding 2,400 miles, crisscrossing the state from one end to the other and visiting with horticulture friends in botanic gardens and their personal "garden variety" gardens.

Fresno Demonstration Garden

In short, I have scratched and sniffed with some of the best gardeners in the state, and in hundreds of wonderfully honest gardens in diverse settings we have uncovered some of California's toughest plants thriving in near utter neglect.

THE LATE GARDEN AUTHOR HENRY MITCHELL WROTE that "there are only two kinds of people—those who garden and those who do not." But most of us are basically lawn mowers and shrub pruners, with maybe some potted plants on the patio to watch through the window while we are glued to Reality TV. Mowing and pruning are to gardening what smoothing a bedspread is to housekeeping.

Yet most of us remember grandmothers and aunts, dads and uncles, and neighbors who grew all sorts of interesting stuff. Truth is, we need to grow something—anything—that depends on us at least a little bit, or as my friend Russell Studebaker, world famous horticulturist from Tulsa, Oklahoma, says, "We'd just as well be sittin' around polishin' our silverware."

Reasons for Not Gardening

There are at least eight very simple and understandable reasons why good people, even flower lovers, often have miserable gardens:

- Too tied up with family, work, church, meetings, sports, housework, the Internet, and other distractions.
- The weather won't cooperate when the mood for gardening strikes.
- Our bodies ache. The easy chair by the TV beckons.
- Bugs and critters unnerve us, and *who knows* what mosquitoes might be carrying this year.
- Too many rules piled on us by garden experts are daunting, almost guaranteeing we'll mess up.
- Neighbors talk about us—and who wants to look like a fanatic?
- Bugs and blights ruin our best efforts, and even "natural" pesticides are expensive and fussy.
- Plants die anyway, no matter what we do or how hard we try. So we give up.

There is a simple solution to all the above: Find and plant things that grow themselves whether we tend to them or not! And arrange them in combinations that make neighbors at least think we know what we are doing.

Selecting the Plants for This Book

Of the thousands of plants we can possibly grow, including old favorites and exciting new cultivars, the plants in this book are the compilation of years of observation by me and many of California's top garden gurus. For a plant to "make the cut" it had to:

- Grow in all or most of the populated areas of California.
- Possess strong values, such as beauty, better flavor or fragrance, multiple-season effects, or be native or heirloom.
- Grow in ordinary dirt with minimum watering or fertilizing.

"Blue Tree" at Cornerstone Festival of Gardens, Sonoma

MASTER GARDENERS ARE MEN AND WOMEN who have been given many hours of intensive training in all aspects of home horticulture by Extension Service professionals. In return, they have given an equal number of hours (sometimes many, many more) teaching others about gardening. They are the "take it to the streets" arm of the university. Find out more, or how you can become involved, by calling your county Extension Service office, or check out **www.mastergardeners.org**.

- Tolerate local climate and weather extremes, including heat, drought, rain, fog, and wind.
- Resist insect pests and diseases.
- Not require the gardener to have a horticulture degree—these plants all but grow themselves.
- Be "no fuss" and easy to groom in the off-season.
- Be easy to find at local garden centers or through mail-order sources.

Not a Lot of How-To

This book is for both beginners and "old hands" who just want pretty plants, without all the fuss. You won't find a lot of horticultural instruction in this book, for two reasons: It is covered thoroughly in nearly every other California gardening book, and most of these plants simply don't need a lot of care. Most require only three acts on your part: Dig a decent hole, plant them "green side up," and water to get them established. As San Diego's beloved and highly pragmatic Extension horticulturist Vincent Lazaneo put it, "It's easy to have something flowering every week of the year. All you have to do is water."

"Best for Beginners" and "Kinda Tricky" Lists

One gardener's wildflower is another gardener's weed.

Because of personal experiences, no two gardeners will ever agree on a list of "best" and "worst" plants. Some plants are so easy to grow they're considered common or weedy, but are acceptable "intro" plants for beginner gardeners—and often cherished long after their success has started to wear thin. On the other hand, some very popular plants are "kinda tricky" by needing a little extra care, and may frustrate beginners who don't know about preventive maintenance.

Lotusland Harlot

You can grow them all, from both lists, but don't say I didn't warn you about some of them!

The Myth of the Five-Dollar Hole

I was taught in college that it is better to put a fifty-cent plant in a five-dollar hole, than a five-dollar plant in a fifty-cent hole. This meant fluffing up your soil with organic matter—bark, compost, peat moss—and is often considered crucial to early plant survival.

However, California soils are very different from other parts of the country. Without getting into detail, most of the plants in this book simply grow in plain, unamended native dirt—which is what they will encounter once their roots hit the sides of their original hole. Adding too much organic matter can lead to problems, by causing soils to hold water during wet seasons, dry out quickly, and keep roots in a small area.

Most landscapers now add little or no soil amendments, preferring to use plants that grow well in native soils; however, in most gardens, a moderate approach usually works best. Think "crackers in chili"—a bowl of chili usually doesn't need any crackers at all, but a handful of crumbled crackers can fluff it up and cool it down; more than that turns it into mush.

A rule of thumb for how much organic matter to add: for trees, tough shrubs, and bulbs, add little or none; for perennials and annuals, add a 1- to 2-inch layer of new material over the native soil and stir it in. No amount of soil improvement will overcome bad plant selection or poor planting. But you don't have to overdo the soil preparation thing. SPECIAL NOTE: Slightly loosen tightly knit roots from store-bought plants at planting time.

Mulch, Mulch, Mulch—It Makes a Difference

Covering the soil with a blanket of porous material keeps the soil surface from packing and crusting in heavy rains, shades and cools the soil in the summer (like a hat on a bare head), reduces rapid temperature changes during sunny days and cool nights, prevents many weed seeds from getting the sun they need to sprout, and keeps things looking neat. Landscape fabrics do a fair job, but natural mulches of leaves, compost, or bark "feed" the soil as they decay.

A rule of thumb for how much mulch to use: Spread your preferred material over the area deep enough to completely cover the soil, then add that much more to compensate for settling and natural composting. It is best to use the mulch evenly over the root area under shrubs and around flowers—don't pile it up around trunks and stems like a mound. Refresh once or twice a year as needed.

Two Rules for Composting

It's too hard trying to remember all the tricks to composting: small particle sizes, correct carbon-nitrogen ratio, thermophilic bacteria, bins an exact size, turning and aerating, and all the rest of that stuff—*bleccchhh!* If you want to get in a race with someone, call your county Extension Service office for a handout on ways to speed things up. They include:

- Mix a little green stuff, including grass clippings and vegetable scraps, even non-seeding weeds, with brown stuff (decaying manure, shredded autumn leaves, etc.), or add a little nitrogen fertilizer.
- Keep the pile moist but not wet (moisture is needed by good bacteria).
- Turn the pile occasionally to mix and fluff it up (air is also needed for good bacterial action).
- Chop big stuff into smaller particles.

As anyone with a leaf pile will attest, there are really only two rules for composting: **Stop throwing that stuff away, and pile it up somewhere.** The rest is finesse. Better yet, forget the rules—just do it!

Water Wisely

No question, there is a chronic water shortage; even in areas that have plenty of rainfall it is hard to get it all into the pipes at one time. By gardening with "water wise" practices, you can reduce your watering needs by 20 to 50 percent, plus improve the health of your plants.

"Drought tolerant" means a plant can go a little longer than you expect without supplemental water. Yet there is no good advice for watering tough plants—after all, many can survive on rainfall alone. But sooner or later even

the toughest plants will need a little help—if not for survival, then for better growth and attractiveness.

Potted plants, summer annuals, and a nicely maintained lawn need watering fairly often, but well-established trees and shrubs barely need any water at all; watering woody plants and perennials too often keeps roots shallow and needy. Still, because mature trees and large shrubs create cool, energy-saving shade (and increase property value), take care of them. Occasional deep soakings—really deep—will encourage deep, strong roots.

Tried-and-true water saving tips:

- Landscape with the right plant, in the right place, to begin with—choose drought tolerant plants, grouped together based on their water needs.
- Reduce the size of your lawn.
- Control weeds, which sap a lot of moisture from the soil.
- Mulch to retain moisture (note: keep mulches off tree and shrub trunks to reduce bark diseases and discourage gnawing mice from making themselves at home).
- Soaker hoses and drip irrigation are convenient for beds and individual plants—as long as you keep them clear, not clogged with water mineral build-up (emitters clog easily; try using 1 gallon-per-hour sizes—good luck). Also keep sprinklers working well.
- Water deeply, not frequently; have sprinklers cycle on and off a few minutes apart to reduce runoff and increase infiltration. Aerate the lawn to help water soak in more quickly. For pots and beds, water twice, an hour or so apart, to give the first watering time to soak in; the second watering really pushes it down deep.
- Minimize evaporation and waste by watering in early morning or early evening, and not during windy conditions.

- Water at the base of plants, not overhead, to reduce evaporation.
- Water less often when it's rainy, cool/cold, humid, cloudy, or if the days are short and the sun is low. Water more often when it's windy, hot, and dry.

Remember that water does not necessarily equal love—too much may not be a good thing. For the plants in this book, too much water (like too much fertilizer) may be worse than none at all. When in doubt, DON'T water.

Feed Plants for Quality, Not Quantity

Most of the people telling you to feed, feed, feed your plants either sell fertilizer or are in a race with someone in a plant-nut club or society. Many tough plants can go for years without fertilizers—just look around and see for yourself. But giving them an occasional feeding can boost their performance and invigorate them with healthier leaves, stems, roots, and flowers.

All plants want is a little pick-me-up from time to time, particularly with nitrogen, phosphorous, and potassium (N, P, K—the "big three," whose numbers are on fertilizer bags). In general for lawns and generic green foliage plants, it's okay to use a fertilizer with a higher first number (nitrogen); for flowering or fruiting plants, use one with a higher middle number (phosphorous).

However—and this is a biggee—because of several soil chemistry issues not worth going into, those generic "big three" N, P, K fertilizers aren't quite enough for quality plants. California soils need a little extra of what are called

Soil pH—Not a Big Deal?

Hate to bust a big myth, but only farmers, horticulturists, and plant hobbyists need to pay close attention to all aspects of their soils. Most gardeners really don't. You can add stuff to neutralize or acidify soils (sulphur, iron sulfate), but not much is practical for the long run. And in garden soils, ups and downs can be worse for plants than no change at all. For most gardens, the best solution is to simply grow locally adapted plants, avoiding the relatively few plants that really do care about pH.

But for detailed information about your soil type and what (if anything) can be done about it, check with your county Extension office, then follow those recommendations as far as you can without going over the edge. Just remember that what we do to soil pH rarely changes things appreciably or for very long.

secondary or "trace" nutrients such as iron, zinc, magnesium, and calcium, which typical all-purpose fertilizers do not contain. Look for them on the label, or ask for them at a garden center.

And don't underestimate the value of compost and natural fertilizers—*they work*, often better in the long run than synthetics. Just don't ever overdo it—plants don't need or appreciate the extra buzz. "Lean and mean" is the best way to keep plants growing but still tough.

Bugs and Blights—Oh My!

Snails, birds, ants, gophers, rats, squirrels, spiders, and giant grasshoppers are just part of life here. Some we simply don't understand or they are more nuisance than pest—some are actually beneficial in ways we may not notice, or appreciate (snakes eat ground squirrels).

Controls, for the most part, work best with an established routine, like shaving—do it early, do it often, and expect to continue doing it. There are commercial trappers, poison people, and even a few "catch and release" folks out there, and lots of clever "exclusion" devices, but no really effective repellents. Barn owls living in boxes on poles really do eat a lot of rodents, but the varmints just increase anyway. Copper strips attached to boards around the bottom of the fence can repel slugs to some extent, and slug baits containing iron phosphate can work so well your garden will smell like a fishing boat for a few days.

The best overall approach simply involves using several different easy practices:

- Choose pest-resistant plants to begin with.
- Replace problem plants (it ain't like y'all are married!).
- Plant well—this goes a long ways towards healthy plants.
- Fertilize lightly, not heavily (overfed plants are weak and tender).
- Water deeply and infrequently, and only when plants really need it.
- Remove diseased plants or plant parts, or damaged parts that can lead to diseases.
- Encourage beneficial insects, birds, even spiders and lizards, which eat pests.

- Hand pick or wash insects off plants with soapy water.
- Use traps, baits, repellents, or other non-toxic measures.

Finally, if your shrubs or flowers have small bugs or blots, spots, raggedy edges, and the like, try this: Take three big steps back from the affected plant, take off your glasses, and *bingo!*—most of those kinds of worries disappear.

These guidelines are nothing new—just good practices used by gardeners for many centuries. As one contributor to an Internet gardening forum put it, on using pesticides indiscriminately, "With the monarch butterfly population crashing, honeybees disappearing, and bird populations in decline, is it really more important to have nice roses?" Bugs and critters are not going to inherit the earth—they already own it. Get used to them.

Before spending a lot of money on useless or dangerous "snake oil" remedies, contact your county Extension service for good advice. And repeat to yourself this mantra: *If you can't fix it, flee it, or fight it, flow with it.*

Landscaping Made Easy

There ain't a whole lot that you *have* to do to be a pretty successful gardener, beyond choosing tough plants and planting them *fairly well*. After that, watering wisely, occasional fertilizing, and a little trimming are the only routine things most good gardeners really need to do.

Still, how you arrange plants determines both how they look, and how they work together.

Keep in mind that cities usually have guidelines or regulations on the types of landscaping allowed in front yards, especially in architecturally controlled neighborhoods. The persistent gardener can usually transform this stilted approach slowly over time.

To ape a cliché, there are no cliché plants, only cliché gardeners. Here are some simple tricks to getting more use out of your garden, with less effort, and to avoid trouble down the road:

- **LOOK** at your garden. Can you see it from the house, or do you have to walk

out to the street and turn around to see it? Plant stuff you can see from your own point of view.

- **WANDER** around your home grounds. If the walk or path is uncomfortable to you, it's even worse for visitors.
- **LESSEN** your chores. Lose whatever needs too much mowing, watering, weeding, whatever-ing. Make your lawn smaller with mulches and groundcovers.
- **LOSE** a plant that is killing your enthusiasm—most flowers are just passing through.
- **SIT** in your garden. No place? Make a place that is comfortable in all seasons and weather. Do something to make it smell and sound nice, too.
- **LOOK UP.** Get your eyes off the ground with a trellis, arbor, or other "vertical" feature.
- **FLAT IS BORING.** Add a raised berm or planter, sunken garden, or tree house.
- **ADD THESE:** Water feature, evening lighting and fragrance, dining area, music.
- **ENJOY.** Don't abide taste-makers or plant snobs. It's your yard, your garden, your lifestyle.

Zone Denial

This book does not include Hardiness Zone maps for a reason: They are guidelines at best, and you can find local experts— including neighbors, if you care to meet them—who can help you better understand where you are gardening.

The USDA Hardiness Zone map is based on "average low temperatures," which are often way off base in California; the American Horticultural Society's Heat Zone Map, based on average high temperatures, is also not entirely useful by itself. The hallowed Sunset Map is a great reference—it considers a broad range of factors, including winter

Watts Towers

minimums, summer highs, elevation, proximity to coast or mountains, rainfall, humidity, aridity, and growing season—but doesn't take into account the difference between front and back yards, or an individual gardener's enthusiasm.

What we need is to overlay all three maps, plus a wind map, rainfall map, fog map, miserably poor soil map, and a "too tired to garden" map. Then we'll have some useful information!

Keeping in mind that what flies in Berkeley may fry in Bakersfield, and what thrives in Sacramento may sulk in Santa Maria's fog, I have kept three areas in mind for all plant choices: So-Cal, Bay area, and Central Valley, with a nod to desert areas and lower mountain elevations. Any more detail than this can get tedious, except to hardcore horticulturists—and this book is not for them anyway!

Wildflowers for California Gardens

California has some of the most amazing native plants in the world—many found *only* here. Many dozens have been found to be fantastic "garden quality" plants, and when brought into landscapes they lend a special "sense of place" feeling of authentic California. Many of the toughest and most beautiful native trees, shrubs, groundcovers, perennials, and annuals are scattered throughout this book.

In addition to using and enjoying native plants as part of a "regular" garden, many can be planted where mowing is impossible or undesirable such as in a large meadow or on a hillside or ditch bank. The idea of a wildflower garden is a romantic one but must be done in a practical manner, or neighbors and perhaps city ordinances will step in.

Keep in mind that there are two groups of wildflowers: native wildflowers, which are plants that have always grown in California; and "naturalized" wildflowers which are freely seeding plants that were brought to California either on purpose or accidentally and have spread on their own. Also note that many wildflowers, both native and non-native, can be considered weeds in some garden settings.

For more detailed information on native plants and wildflowers, look for a local wildflower or native plant group (find them through your Extension Service office), or visit the website of the California Native Plant Society (**www.cnps.org**).

You Might Be a California Gardener If...

For the uninitiated, here are some general guidelines to tell if you are a California gardener:

- You don't "landscape"—you *arrange*.
- Your tool shed is starting to look like a half-million dollar investment property.
- The !##*!! pesky Argentine ants are in your ears when you wake up in the morning.
- You know what "fog drip" is and/or your city's school was closed because of a fog-out.
- Your garden center checkout employee has six body piercings and none are visible.
- Gas costs more than your shrubs.
- You can't remember if growing pot is illegal.
- Both you and your dog or cat have therapists.
- *Ser naco es chido*—being tacky is cool.
- The familiar phrase "invasive exotic" means you feel sneaky about still growing ivy.
- If you have ever thought about eating the snails in your garden with garlic butter.
- The neighborhood cell tower is dressed like a metal palm or pine.
- On a clear day you can see the mountains.
- You feel guilty for owning a redwood deck—because you've visited its forest home.
- Xeriscape—okay, okay, you GET it already!
- Your bumper sticker says "I Brake for Agapanthus."
- You know how many bags of compost your car can hold, and you've cleaned it with a leaf blower.
- You worry about losing your tennis bracelet when digging in the dirt.
- Your garden has black spaghetti drip irrigation tubes running everywhere.
- You can amuse yourself for an hour with a garden hose.
- It gets so dry the trees start whistling for the dog.
- You can grow prickly pear and crape myrtles side by side.
- You can't mow or blow leaves on certain days because of a noise pollution ordinance.
- You spend more money trying to grow tomatoes than they'd cost at the store.
- High winds always arrive right after you have planted a 5-gallon tree.
- You don't really understand the Sunset plant zones map.
- Your shrubs were selected according to fire resistance.
- The freeway has a better-maintained irrigation system than your own yard.
- A hummer is a vehicle, not a bird.

Annuals
THAT ENDURE

Bedding plants and annuals are used for fast color or screening, as container plants and hanging baskets, as vegetables or herbs, and in long-blooming masses or as specimen plants. They provide all-season "color bridges" as perennials flush in and out of show, can give solid color in the winter or summer (even in the shade), and add interest to shrubbery when it is out of season.

It's a given, in the gardening world, that a lot of popular plants live for only a short time and then die no matter what you do. Regardless of how long they can potentially live, whether they are true annuals (grow, flower, set seed, and die in a season), tender perennials that just don't love the climate, or tropical plants that are cheap or just easier to buy every year, they are usually grouped together.

But they are so enjoyable or productive that gardeners continue to replant them, year after year, in spite of the trouble and expenses of time, extra effort, money, and maintenance. In all but Southern California's coastal areas, there are two seasons for these annual plants: the "warm season" from March to November, with long, warm days; and the "cool season" from November through February, with short, cool days and cool or even frosty nights or short periods of freezing weather. In certain areas, long, hot summers can cause even some warm-season annuals to burn out from exhaustion, and pruning and fertilizing can't rejuvenate them; but when temperatures cool off in the fall months, these same annuals can be replanted.

Still, a surprising number are tougher than others, being unusually tolerant of local weather, soils, pests, and neglectful gardeners. Some reseed themselves to "come back" many years on their own; others have seeds that are easily saved from year to year or are readily available at garden centers or through mail order. A few are hard to grow from seed, but cuttings are easily rooted or they can be purchased as rooted plants.

What makes most bedding plants and other annuals high maintenance is the soil preparation often required at planting time, plus the regular fertilization, mulching, weed control, and especially watering during extremely sunny, windy, or hot spells (even in winter).

Soil preparation for annuals involves digging your soil as best you can to at least a shovel's depth, and adding a little stuff to your native dirt. It is very important for short-lived plants to get started right by working in organic matter such as compost, soil conditioner, peat moss, composted manure, or potting soil. This helps roots grow quickly and deeply, and helps hold moisture and nutrients. Generally, a layer of organic matter 2 or 3 inches deep, laid over the previously dug area and then tilled in, will work wonders throughout most of the

Periwinkles

season. It is better to use a little each of two or three different kinds of organic matter, for a total of 2 to 4 inches, than a lot of just one kind. Don't overdo this, or plants will dry out or flop around in the too-loose soil.

Fertilization means adding a small amount of a balanced or all-purpose fertilizer—organic or natural, if you can get it—to your soil during soil preparation or at planting time, and again every month or two (or three) to replace what has washed away. Most gardeners overdo it by adding too much at a time, causing plants to become "leggy" or grow too fast, resulting in poor flowering, or making plants more susceptible to weather, moisture problems, and pest pressures. A general rule of thumb, regardless of what kind of fertilizer you use, is to apply no more than 1 pound (about a pint jar full) of fertilizer for every 100 square feet (10 by 10 feet, 4 by 25, 5 by 20, etc.) of planting area. Adding more fertilizer later in the growing season is often helpful but never overdo it. Most gardeners would agree that using a slow-acting, "timed-release" fertilizer is cheaper and easier, and better for your plants, than a hit-or-miss liquid feeding every few weeks.

Mulching simply means covering the newly worked soil with a layer of shredded or chipped bark or compost to keep the sun from overheating the soil, to keep the soil from crusting over after hard rains or watering, and to slow the germination of weed seeds. Synthetic fabric mulches do a fair job of weed control but do not decay and "feed" the soil or its worms. A rule of thumb for how much mulch to use is to see how much it takes of your favorite kind to completely but barely cover the soil and then add that much more to compensate for packing and natural composting.

Weed control—sorry about this, but it's true—is usually done by "shaving" them out of the soil with a sharp hoe, mulching to keep seeds from sprouting, or, in worst-case scenarios, using chemical weed killers—which are not always dependable or safe for other plants. For information on weed control, consult your Extension Service home garden advisor, a Master Gardener, or a dependable, trained garden center employee to show you products that list your kinds of weeds and your kinds of plants on the labels. Note: Pulling, chopping, tilling, etc. disturbs the soil—bringing more weed seeds to the surface and creating conditions for blown-in weed seeds to get a better "footing."

Watering is a given for even tough annuals, especially when it is hot and dry in the summer or during long spells of sunny, windy weather, including in the winter. Some annuals can get by with just occasional soakings, while others need regular, consistent watering; annuals in containers need more watering than those in the ground. How often to water and how much are variable; the rule of thumb is to water only when needed, but do it twice—once to "set up" the soil and a second time, a few minutes after the first, to really soak it in so it will last longer. Drip irrigation, while not the most effective way to water, is often the easiest, and water-conservative approach.

Note on Pest Control

Most of these plants have few pests, practically none that are major. Occasional leaf spots and minor insect or mite infestations can make some plants look bad, but it is still a good idea to avoid pesticides whenever possible in order to protect bees, butterflies, and other beneficial creatures. When possible, choose a "natural" product such as insecticidal soap, biological worm control, neem oil, or diatomaceous earth to control minor insect pests. And be prepared to simply pull up annuals that are suffering under intolerable problems—something else is always waiting to go in that hole! Also be aware that overwatering or overfeeding can cause tough plants to be more susceptible to problems.

Tender, Hardy, or Half-Hardy

To gardeners, the term *annual* doesn't give enough information. Optimists think it means a plant that will grow quickly for fast rewards, if just for a short while. Pessimists realize that the plant in question is going to die sooner, rather than later. So, to get the very most out of an annual's short life, when is the best time to go for the gusto? Stick with me on this:

Some annual plants love hot weather, but freeze in the winter or suffer in mild winter areas; some prefer cool weather, and even tolerate frosts or light freezes. These plants have traditionally been grouped as "warm season" or "cool season" annuals, respectively.

But what about those that dislike both cool weather *and* intense heat? Many very popular, long-lived tropical perennials freeze in cold winters; some normally tough northern plants die in summer heat. *It's the same with annuals.*

So a third group of annuals needs to be recognized—half-hardy annuals—those that love warm weather, hate cool weather, but sulk, wear out, or just plain die in intense, prolonged summer heat. They can be planted in earliest spring for several months of enjoyment and if they burn out in midsummer, a gardener can replant new ones after the heat is past, for many months of fall performance.

That is the way I address plants in this chapter, which are henceforth designated as *tender, hardy,* or *half-hardy*:

TA   Tender Annual: Needs summer heat—plant in the spring or early summer

HA   Hardy Annual: Needs cool weather and tolerates frost or light freezes—plant in the fall

HHA   Half-Hardy Annual: Needs warmth but suffers in extreme heat—plant in spring and/or late summer

 ## Best for Beginners:

- *Ageratum*
- *California Poppy*
- *Celosia*
- *Coleus*
- *Gomphrena*
- *Moss Rose*
- *Ornamental Sweet Potato*
- *Pansy*
- *Salvia*
- *Sweet Alyssum* (easy to grow)

Kinda Tricky:

- *Impatiens* (need watering, risk root rot)
- *Marigolds* (spider mites)
- *Sweet Alyssum* (weedy)
- *Zinnias* (leaf disease)

Ageratum
Ageratum houstonianum
Sun (TA)

"Floss flower" is a popular old plant for spring-to-fall flowers, very reliable in beds or containers.

FLOWER: Broad heads of small powder-puffs in blue, pink, lavender-blue, or white are held above the foliage, sometimes on sturdy stems bred to cut for flower arrangements.

PLANT: Slightly spreading mound of medium-green pointy-oval leaves with slightly toothed edges, that can tolerate all but the worst cold and heat; it can overwinter in warm-winter areas, but may have to be replanted in midsummer in hot regions for a fall display.

INTERESTING KINDS: Several strains have been introduced, but you are mostly at the mercy of whatever local retailers or mail-order companies offer. Look or ask for either dwarf kinds ('Blue Danube', 'Blue Surf') or 'Blue Horizon' which is a long-stemmed cut-flower type.

Balfour's Touch-Me-Not
Impatiens balfourii
Part shade or shade (HHA)

This somewhat hard-to-find shade plant is a prolific re-seeder that can fill any moist shaded area for many summers to come. My "start" came from a garden friend in Menlo Park, and has been passed along to countless others.

FLOWER: Lavender-and-white flowers with a prominent backward-facing spur appear to float above the dark foliage. Seedpods spring open to fling seeds at the slightest touch.

PLANT: Moderately dense shrubby plant 2 to 3 feet tall and wide with deep green oval leaves. Succulent stems are easy to prune or break off to encourage more bushiness. Unwanted seedlings are easy to pull.

INTERESTING KINDS: Balsam (*I. balsamina*) is another, larger-leaf touch-me-not with pink, white, or orange flowers close to the main stem, and small oblong seedpods.

Black-Eyed Susan
Rudbeckia hirta
Sun or very light shade (HA)

This very familiar prairie wildflower is one of the best butterfly and cutting flowers to ever grow on a sunny hillside or in a meadow.

FLOWER: Thin, sunflower-like rays of mostly golden yellow on long, stiff stems in the spring and early summer, usually with dark cones or "noses."

PLANT: Low-growing rosettes with rough, slightly hairy leaves, and several many-branched flowering stems sent up in early spring through summer. Prefers fall seeding in poor but well-drained soils.

INTERESTING KINDS: The native species is pretty enough but rarely available except in wildflower mixes. But the double-flowered Gloriosa strain has 6- to 7-inch-wide flowers that are banded with orange, yellow, burgundy. 'Irish Eyes' has 3-inch yellow flowers with green cones. Also look for 'Goldilocks', 'Toto', and 'Becky'.

Calendula
Calendula officinalis
Sun (HA)

"Pot marigold" is an old-world edible plant, grown (or harvested from the wild) as a cooked vegetable or for making wine. Its large flowers bloom dependably over the winter everywhere and into the summer in cool-summer areas.

FLOWER: Prettier than they are tasty, these daisy-like flowers have thickly-packed (double) petals of bright yellow or orange, though some newer varieties are softer pastels of cream and apricot. Removing faded flowers makes plants more attractive, and cuts down on prolific seed production. Flowers are larger on plants that are watered occasionally.

PLANT: The compact, low-spreading clump has narrow leaves that are somewhat sticky and fragrant when bruised.

INTERESTING KINDS: 'Bon Bon', 'Fiesta', and 'Dwarf Gem' are compact varieties; 'Pacific Beauty' is up to 2 feet tall; 'Touch of Red' is orange with red-brushed tips.

California Poppy
Eschscholzia californica
Sun (HA)

California's official state flower is cheerful, tough, and easy enough for school children to grow them.

FLOWER: Four-petaled flowers are pale to clear yellow or orange, with a satiny sheen. They open only when the sun is out, closing at night and during foggy or overcast weather.

PLANT: Airy, somewhat short-lived perennial with very fine, ferny leaves of blue-green. Usually grown as an annual by sowing seed over loose dirt and watering until seedlings emerge; once established, it's a very tough plant.

INTERESTING KINDS: New strains bred for more general garden use have single, double, or frilled flowers in yellow, orange, red, rose, pink, cream, and white, but may slowly revert to the common species when they reseed.

Castor Bean or Mole Bean
Ricinus communis
Sun or light shade (TA)

This plant is BOLD—big plant, large leaves, perfect for backs of borders or in the center of a bed or large container. Roots are said to repel moles. Warning: The plant reseeds freely, from railroad tracks to natural areas, and its seeds are deadly poisonous. Be careful with it.

FLOWER: Foot-tall stalks of small flowers but marble-size spiny burrs of seed, same color as foliage (again, seeds are toxic—keep away from children).

PLANT: Tall, branching, woody-stemmed, and over 6 feet tall and half as wide, with large lobed leaves up to 2 or more feet across in burgundy or green.

INTERESTING KINDS: 'Sanguineus' (blood red), 'Zanzibarensis' (solid green); 'Carmencita Red' and 'Carmencita Pink' bear beautiful foliage and brightly-colored seed heads. 'Dwarf Red Spire' is under 6 feet tall.

Celosia
Celosia argentea
Sun (TA)

These plants will grow in gravel, and can reseed themselves in some areas.

FLOWER: Cockscomb (Cristata group) has bizarre, fissured, rounded heads up to a foot across of velvety, fan-shaped, wavy flower clusters of yellow, orange, crimson, purple, and red. Plume cockscomb or prince's feather (Plumosa group) has smaller, pointed plumes of red, pink, golden, or white. Spicata types have long pointed flower heads of pink or pink and white.

PLANT: Pointed oval leaves of medium green, sometimes with a reddish tinge, up to 2 feet or more tall and half as wide. Use as specimen, in combinations, or massed.

INTERESTING KINDS: ' Flamingo Feather' has tapered/pointed flower heads of silvery-buff blushed with pink; 'Flamingo Purple' has dark reddish-green leaves and purple spikes; 'Pink Candle' has rose pink spikes; 'New Look' is a tall-growing type with deep bronzy-purple foliage and intense red heads; the Bombay series are suitable for cutting.

Cleome or Spider Flower
Cleome hassleriana
Sun or light shade (HHA)

Tall fluffy plants with marijuana-like leaves. Good cut flower that wilts when first cut but perks up in water. Excellent butterfly and hummingbird plant, great in masses behind other flowers or combined with bold texture plants in large containers.

FLOWER: Airy heads 6 inches wide, loosely arranged with open flowers with spidery "cat whisker" stamens and long narrow seed pods, in white, pink, or dusty purple.

PLANT: Four-foot branching shrubby plants with palm-like foliage that is sticky and has a not-so-nice aroma when cut, and small prickly thorns. Seeds sown in spring are slow to germinate, but do finally come up. Can reseed prolifically.

INTERESTING KINDS: 'Helen Campbell' is snow white. There are a number of Queen varieties (cherry, pink, rose, purple, mauve, ruby indicate color). The Sparkler series has large flower heads on compact, bush plants under 4 feet tall.

Coleus

Solenostemon scutellarioides

Shade, part shade, part sun (TA)

This old-fashioned Victorian plant has been gussied up and made sturdier, with bigger leaves, showier flowers, and more sun tolerance.

FLOWER: Up to foot-long spikes of blue or lavender flowers at the tip of every stem; some gardeners remove the spikes to encourage more leaf production; I think the blooms provide an important foil to the big, garish foliage. Your call.

PLANT: Upright or cascading plants with square stems and big bold leaves, with a tremendous variation in shape, leaf color, and pattern—a spilled box of crayons can't begin to compete (an Internet "word search" for coleus can make you go blind).

INTERESTING KINDS: New 'Kong' Coleus has huge leaves (needs shade); 'Plum Parfait' is just one of many with full-sun tolerance.

Coreopsis

Coreopsis species

Sun (HA, HHA)

This common prairie wildflower, a close relative of black-eyed Susan and sunflowers, "tames" very well in urban flower borders, containers, and butterfly or cut-flower gardens.

FLOWER: Cheerful yellow disks 2 or more inches across from mid-spring through midsummer.

PLANT: Short, stocky clump of linear foliage appears in early winter and peters out after flowering.

INTERESTING KINDS: Tickseed (*C. grandiflora*) is a very short-lived clumpy perennial with solid yellow flowers that reseeds itself well; *C. tinctoria* is an airy 4-foot, openly-branched plant with finely-divided, almost ferny leaves, and many small flowers that are yellow with a reddish aura around the flower center; compact varieties are available. A similar species is calliopsis (*C. basalis*).

Cosmos
Cosmos species
Sun (HHA)

This showstopper is one of the most impressive flowers of the spring and fall, and reseeds to the point of being a nuisance.

FLOWER: Showy, single, flat daisy-like flowers of pink, burgundy, or white (*C. bipinnatus*), or deep orange or yellow (*C. sulphureus*).

PLANT: Large branching plant with deep green, divided, marigold-like leaves; tends to look ragged after a few weeks of flowering. Cut old plants down and shake their seed onto the ground for a spectacular fall show. Thin excess plants in the spring and summer.

INTERESTING KINDS: *Cosmos sulphureus* is a tall annual up to 7 feet with yellow-centered, yellow or orange single flowers. Bright Lights and Klondike strains are half as big as the species with 3$^1/_2$-inch flowers in yellow and orange; 'Sunny Red' has orange-red flowers.

Forget-Me-Not
Myosotis sylvatica
Light shade or shade (HA)

Don't let this being the state flower of Alaska throw you—it's also a very fine over-wintering annual for all of California.

FLOWER: Tiny but showy "true blue" flowers each with a white eye, loosely arranged on narrow stems held just above the foliate. Blooms for a long time, from late winter to late spring, and then sets seeds that can invade nearby moist areas of your garden.

PLANT: Clump of softly hairy leaves the size of an index finger, with smaller leaves growing up flower stalks. Seeds and expands enough to make a good shade groundcover.

INTERESTING KINDS: 'Blue Ball' and 'Royal Blue Improved' are improvements in general appearance and flowering over the wild kinds.

31

Globe Amaranth
Gomphrena globosa
Sun (TA)

This heat-loving plant is a choice companion to other flowers for its airy, branched growth and round flowers. Super easy to dry for long-lasting flower arrangements, fair butterfly plant.

FLOWER: Bristly, round, button-like clover heads up to an inch long of red, purplish red, pink, or white on long stems up to 3 feet tall. Reasonably good butterfly plant. Long-stemmed flowers retain their color when cut and dried.

PLANT: Often-reseeding summer annual; narrow foliage is very pest resistant. Work this leggy but incredibly drought- and heat-tolerant plant in with other flowers, or mass in a container.

INTERESTING KINDS: 'Strawberry Fields' is tall with red flowers; 'Lavender Lady' is pink; both purplish-red 'Buddy' and white 'Cissy' are compact, good for edging.

Johnny Jump-Ups
Viola tricolor
Sun (HA)

Favorite "old garden" winter annual, planted in the fall to flower through the worst winter. Perfect filler for containers, borders, or mass planting over dormant spring bulbs

FLOWER: Sweetly fragrant, purple and yellow pansies about the size of a quarter, fall to late spring.

PLANT: Floppy many-branched mounds of small roundish leaves, to a foot or more tall and wide, set out in the fall or late winter as transplants. Reseeds.

INTERESTING KINDS: There are many great named varieties, but the Panola and Sorbet series are hybrids between small Johnny-jump-ups and larger pansies with larger flowers; compact plants, in many hues of white, yellow, apricot, blue, purple, and others.

Larkspur
Consolida ambigua
Winter sun, summer light shade (HA)

Larkspur is like a miniature delphinium, with similar but less-substantial spikes of smaller flowers, but still good for a spiky flowerbed effect and cut flowers. It is a great companion to iris and other late spring or early summer perennials.

FLOWER: Narrow, dense spikes of half-inch or longer, interesting violet-like flowers of deep or pale blue, pink, and white, produced in spring and early summer. (Look closely—the inner part of each flower resembles a bunny face, ears and all.) Some varieties have double flowers.

PLANT: Airy, branching 4- to 5-foot-tall plant with delicate ferny leaves grows best over the winter; old-timey single varieties reseed prolifically

INTERESTING KINDS: Giant Imperial and Regal strains are many-branched with larger flowers than the species; 'Steeplechase' has large flowers and is the most heat tolerant.

Lobelia
Lobelia erinus
Sun or part shade (HHA)

Blue is such a hard color to find for the summer garden, but this bedding and container plant fits the bill with electric gusto.

FLOWER: Small, flared-lip tubular flowers of blue, cobalt, white, pink, or reddish purple bloom constantly if plants are in good soil that is kept moist.

PLANT: Compact or trailing plants with small green or bronze-green leaves. Can be grown outdoors all winter where winters are mild; in hotter areas start seed indoors in late winter to set out for spring and early summer flowering.

INTERESTING KINDS: Compact 'Cambridge Blue' is soft blue; 'Crystal Palace' is intense deep blue; trailing 'Sapphire' is popular in containers and hanging baskets; Color Cascade is a series of floriferous long-trailing types; Riviera is a new series of nicely compact plants.

Marigold

Tagetes species

Sun (HHA)

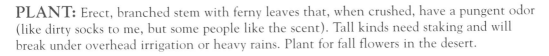

This Mexican native plant was only narrowly beaten out by the rose as America's Floral Emblem.

FLOWER: Round, flat, daisy-like or dense balls of yellow, orange, gold, maroon, and combinations, produced in warm weather until frost. Long lasting as cut flowers and the single kinds are great for butterflies.

PLANT: Erect, branched stem with ferny leaves that, when crushed, have a pungent odor (like dirty socks to me, but some people like the scent). Tall kinds need staking and will break under overhead irrigation or heavy rains. Plant for fall flowers in the desert.

INTERESTING KINDS: The line between the large African or American type (*T. erecta*) and smaller French type (*T. patula*) has been blurred by hybridizers and now the market is wide open for any kind that suits your fancy.

Melampodium

Melampodium paludosum

Sun (HHA)

It's unfortunate when a lack of a "common" name scares off new gardeners, but this one with a difficult name (it's rarely called "butter daisy") is a "top ten" summer flowering annual for massing in hot, dry parking-lot type garden spots.

FLOWER: Buttery yellow daisies produced in nearly solid sheets, from spring to frost.

PLANT: Mounding plants from 2 to 3 feet with deep green foliage. Requires warm soil and hot sun to flower well. May reseed itself into flower beds that are lightly irrigated.

INTERESTING KINDS: 'Showstar' is compact, under 2 feet tall; 'Medallion' can get over 3 feet tall and half that wide.

34

Mexican Sunflower
Tithonia rotundifolia
Sun (TA)

Big, fast-growing shrubby annual from Mexico that makes a decent tall screen or accent plant that flowers non-stop in heat, drought, and humidity, all the while covered with butterflies and hummingbirds.

FLOWER: Marigold-like flowers up to 4 inches across, brilliant orange or sometimes yellow petals with yellow centers bloom during warm weather. Make very good cut flowers during even very hot weather

PLANT: Large (to 6 feet) multi-branched summer shrub with hand-size, velvety leaves. Reseeds well.

INTERESTING KINDS: 'Sundance' and 'Goldfinger' are more compact, to only 3 or 4 feet; 'Aztec Gold' has apricot gold flowers; 'Fiesta del Sol' is even more compact and blooms earlier than the others.

Moss Rose
Portulaca grandiflora
Sun (TA)

This solid mass of bright flowers opens only for people who are outdoors in the middle of the day. Perfect for rock gardens, edging, and spilling out of containers in hot, dry spots

FLOWER: Compact, inch-wide rose-like clusters of single or double flowers in brilliant red, magenta, pink, and white. Flowers usually open only when warm summer sun shines directly on them

PLANT: Low mounds or trailing plants, 6 inches tall by a foot or more wide, thick with fleshy, cylindrical leaves to an inch long. Reseeds prolifically in hot, dry areas

INTERESTING KINDS: Several improved strains are widely available, including some that remain open longer in the afternoon. Flowering purslane (*P. umbraticola*) has flat leaves and flat, single flowers and is perfect for hanging baskets.

Pansy

Viola wittrockiana

Full winter sun or part shade (HA)

One of the most dependable, carefree fall, winter, and spring flowers for flower beds, edging, or containers.

FLOWER: Flat and up to 4 inches across, in white, blue, purple, red, yellow, orange, with or sometimes without large blotches or a contrasting "eye." Blooms freely from fall to late spring, sometimes longer in cool-summer areas. Removing spent flowers is tedious but can improve flower production.

PLANT: Compact foot-tall mounds of slightly lobed, roundish leaves, requires cool weather for best growth, and generally dies from heat by early summer in hot areas. Best grown from transplants

INTERESTING KINDS: Many hybrid strains and colors are available including big floppy kinds to compact freer-flowering ones, with new ones on the market every year.

Pepper

Capsicum annum

Sun or light shade (TA)

Ornamental peppers are seriously overlooked additions to flower beds, herb gardens, and containers, with a huge array of sizes and fruit colors. Ornamentals are edible, but very hot!

FLOWER: Small, starry white flowers from late spring to frost; fruits are tiny birds-eye to long and thin, from green to yellow, orange, red, purple, and almost black

PLANT: Shrubby summer annuals from 6 inches to 4 feet or taller, many branched with oval leaves of green, purple, or variegated with white or yellow

INTERESTING KINDS: Many varieties of peppers come and go on the market, but note that edible or cooking peppers often have trouble setting a lot of fruit in cool coastal areas. 'Jigsaw' and 'Tri-fetti' have variegated leaves, 'Holiday Flame' and 'Red Missile' bear upright conical fruits that change from pale cream to orange to fiery red; 'Marbles' is a compact plant with marble-shaped fruits.

Periwinkle

Catharanthus roseus

Sun (TA)

Seemingly one of the most drought tolerant plants on Earth, the "sun impatiens" from the hot, dry Madagascar Island off Africa's east coast flowers continually with no care at all except watering in the hottest weather. Also called Madagascar periwinkle.

FLOWER: Flat, five-petaled disks of pure white, pink, or red, sometimes with darker or lighter "eyes," produced in masses atop foliage from spring to frost, more so in hot weather.

PLANT: Compact mound of glossy green foliage up to 2 feet tall, but usually a foot or less. Reseeds prolifically into nearby hot, dry areas; resents water and heavy wet soils. Is often a leggy perennial is mild-winter areas.

INTERESTING KINDS: There are many strains on the market, with more or less creeping or compact habits and larger flowers. The Carpet strain forms a creeping mat. Both the Pacific and Cooler series have large, 2-inch flowers.

Petunia

Petunia hybrids

Sun or light shade (HHA)

Old "grandmother's garden" varieties are not as showy—or as tough—as modern hybrids, but give a wonderful cottage-garden-like element to mixed borders and containers.

FLOWER: Flat or ruffled trumpets of white, pink, red, purple, yellow, or rose, with or without stripes, produced best in cool weather; some strains have flowers 4 inches or more across.

PLANT: Sprawling vine that tolerates cool better than heat. May need "pinching" to thicken scraggly growth. Often reseeds.

INTERESTING KINDS: 'Purple Wave' and others in the Wave series are very dependable through the worst summer weather because of a "self-pruning" habit, which keeps new growth sprouting all the time. The iridescent flowers shed neatly without a gummy mess. Plus, 'Purple Wave' has a very spicy fragrance, day and night.

Salvia
Salvia coccinea
Sun or part shade (HHA)

This summer mainstay is a tender perennial in most of California and is typically used as an annual. It has non-stop showy spikes of flowers from spring to fall, best in hot weather.

FLOWER: Spikes of small but exotic two-lipped trumpets in brilliant red, white, pink, salmon, or interesting combinations. Fantastic butterfly and hummingbird plant.

PLANT: Upright, branching small shrub to 2 feet tall or more, solid green leaves give great contrast to spikes of flowers. Reseeds prolifically everywhere, and can be perennial in mild winter areas.

INTERESTING KINDS: 'Lady in Red', 'Lady in Pink', and 'Lady in White'. 'Coral Nymph' (or 'Cherry Blossom') is nearly white with a coral lower lip

NOTE: The commonly sold scarlet sage (*S. splendens*) is a very tender annual that in hot areas must have shade and needs regular watering.

Silver Shield
Plectranthus argentatus 'Silver Shield'
Shade, light shade, part sun (TA)

Looking much like a large salvia, this tender perennial from Australia is grown as an annual, mostly for its spectacular shimmering gray foliage, especially in shaded borders and containers.

FLOWER: Pale pink or white flowers on foot-long spikes in late summer resemble those of coleus.

PLANT: Large, gray, slightly furry leaves up to 7 inches long have purplish tinged tips and edges, and a silvery sheen. Bushy plants can get 3 feet tall and sprawl 5 feet or more. Will tolerate considerable sun if kept moist, or can simply be set into lightly shaded beds and all but ignored. Easy to root from cuttings.

INTERESTING KINDS: Related to Cuban oregano (*P. amboinicus*), a semi-trailing aromatic plant with roundish leaves (sometimes leaves are chartreuse or have creamy borders or a pink tinge).

Sweet Alyssum
Lobularia maritima
Sun or part shade (HA)

I have been warned to not even mention this very weedy plant—but it's pretty as a groundcover, in containers, as a border along the walk, into the lawn, and on down the street...

FLOWER: Dense clusters with an almost cloying sweet fragrance in the spring and fall; in mild-winter areas it can bloom all year. Freely seeds itself around the garden—and beyond.

PLANT: Low, trailing, many-branched plant up to a foot high, with small, narrow leaves. Plant can be used for erosion control, because they can flower in just six weeks from seed.

INTERESTING KINDS: Hybrid garden varieties, including 'Carpet of Snow' (3 to 4 inches tall) and 'Violet Queen' (5 inches with rich purple flowers) usually revert by seed to common kinds.

Sweet Potato
Ipomoea batatas
Sun or moderate shade (TA)

Ornamental sweet potatoes are grown exclusively for their showy leaves. The fast-growing, trailing (not climbing) vines are unbeatable for attractive foliage in large containers, hanging baskets, or groundcovers. Astounding in masses or entwined with other summer plants.

FLOWER: Not very showy, small "morning glories."

PLANT: Heart-shaped or lobed foliage on long, trailing vines that root as they "run" from spring to frost. Does best in poor soils with low fertility; forms large edible tuberous roots.

INTERESTING KINDS: 'Blackie' has dark burgundy, almost black foliage that is deeply divided; 'Margarita' has shocking chartreuse foliage; 'Pink Frost', while not as vigorous as the others, is variegated white, green, and pink.

Sweet William
Dianthus barbatus
Sun (HA)

One of the few true biennials (grows one year, flowers and sets seed the next, then dies), this antique favorite is grown mostly as an overwintering or "cool season" annual. Its spring flowers are almost electric.

FLOWER: Dense clusters of $1/2$-inch flowers of white, pink, rose, red, purple, or bi-colored are highlighted against a backdrop of dark green leafy bracts, making them seem to glow even more. Double-flowering kinds are easily grown from seed.

PLANT: Sprawling plant with sturdy stems of flat leaves forms an attractive mat over the winter against which spring flowers really stand out.

INTERESTING KINDS: Indian Carpet strain makes a mat only 6 inches high.

Zinnia
Zinnia species
Sun or very light shade (TA)

One of the very best "starter" flowers for kids and adults alike, outstanding for butterflies and cut flowers, best used in masses or behind other plants to hide ugly lower foliage.

FLOWER: Flat or double daisy-like up to 3 or more inches across, in all possible colors, even white (no black), usually with yellow stamen. Produced freely all summer and fall on long stems.

PLANT: Many-branching, compact mounds or tall specimens to 4 feet or more, with pleasing oval leaves, sometimes prone to powdery mildew but plants keep on flowering anyway. Usually reseeds.

INTERESTING KINDS: Narrow-leaf zinnia (*Z. angustifolia*, several good varieties) has loose mounds of gold or white, quarter-size flowers. 'Profusion' series is a fantastic hybrid between *Z. angustifolia* and *Z. elegans*, with compact plants and non-stop nice-size flowers.

Marigolds at Golden Gate Park Conservatory

Note on Seed or Plant Sources

Always shop locally first! While the quality of bedding plants that arrive at garden centers is usually similar from store to store, in many cases—though not always—independent or family-owned garden centers have better-trained staffs who provide more care for plants than some mass-merchandisers, and who are more knowledgeable about the plants and their challenges. Shop at a variety of sources for the best buys and the best service. Mail-order firms often have a larger selection of unusual or old-fashioned plants and seeds. And never overlook the value and fun (and heritage) of swapping seeds and plants with friends and neighbors!

Every seed catalog and most garden books have lots of information on growing annuals, but the best knowledge comes from experience. The plants in this book have been pre-selected by the experience of great "garden variety" gardeners for their ability to be grown throughout the most populated areas of California for many years with little or no effort.

Attractive Edibles

Anyone who's ever had a pansy stick to the roof of his or her mouth has learned the subtle delights of edible flowers. From the sweet, raw-peanut taste of redbud flowers, to battered and fried daylily buds, there's some mighty good eatin' in the garden. Best commonly grown edible flowers to try (when no one is looking): basil, nasturtium, chives, daylily, Johnny jump-ups, pansy, redbud, rose, squash, and violets. There are many more, of course, including a lot of tropical fruits grown as annuals, but you get the flavor.

Rumpelstiltskin's Garden

Remember the old fable of the gnome who wove golden garments from common straw? As I wander around my little cottage garden, I realize that it is a "Rumpelstiltskin" tapestry of sorts.

Because my busy family and I relax in our garden year-round, we've tried to have plants for every season. Ours is a cottage garden, with a style and freedom to grow what we like, where we like, and includes something for all the senses, including taste and touch. Though I've collected rare plants during my travels around the horticulture world, my landscape's backbone is mostly "comfort plants" shared between generous gardeners over many years. Potted plants are everywhere, in a wide variety of containers and hanging baskets, and there are many "hard features" such as bird baths, urns, small statuary, whimsical "yard art," and found objects (rocks, driftwood, etc.).

To outsiders, there is no apparent design, but it has a definite personal layout—best viewed inside-out (from the house, not the street). Our garden is much more than just its plants; the ever-changing scenery is screened from prying eyes of passing joggers with lattice-like fencing, painted teal and pastels to help give a glow of color without being garish. We strew a few comfortable chairs on roomy decks, and have connected each "people space" with meandering paths. There's a waterfall to soothe city sounds, and a large iron bowl on one deck for tending crackling wood fires on chilly evenings.

Having a garden like this increases the likelihood of year-round enjoyment with less work. Such a garden is not a slippery slope—it doesn't have to be an all-consuming obsession!

And just as our "garden of welcome" is alive with birds and other wildlife that delight us with colorful motion and busy chatter, we invite friends over to relax beside our water garden and fire pit. Soon they feel comfortable enough to share stories and laughter that enrich our lives more.

Common straw woven into a golden tapestry. Rumplestiltskin would be proud.

UNBEATABLE
Bulbs

I was raised thinking most bulbs are about the toughest garden plants there are, and to this day I can't imagine my garden without its nearly zero-maintenance beauties. A few very popular kinds, however, won't tolerate either drought or excessive irrigation.

Flowering bulbs and bulb-like perennials that "come and go" with the seasons are sometimes overlooked by new gardeners or folks who want year-round effects. They have traditionally been planted as afterthoughts or in isolated groupings, partly because so many of them have temporary shows and we forget about them the rest of the year. But they can easily be worked into overall landscapes to add or prolong color and provide foliage even in "off" seasons.

Not all the plants in this section are true bulbs. Some are rhizomes, corms, tubers, and other forms of underground structures. In addition to traditional spring-flowering daffodils there are summer-blooming crocosmia, drop-dead gorgeous cannas, and winter-foliaged painted arum.

But what's the difference between bulbs, tubers, rhizomes, and corms anyway? We tend to refer to most of them as "bulbs" and the distinctions can be subtle. All of them are underground structures developed for storing energy, water, and food for new growth, and to sustain the plant during dry spells and dormancy.

Dahlia

Many plants with such structures are native to regions with regular seasonal dry periods. A tuber is a swollen stem, branch, or root (caladium). A corm is a bulbous stem and is annual, forming new corms from buds on the old ones (crocus). A rhizome is a stem also, but can vary in thickness and branching, and can be near the soil surface (iris). A true bulb is a modified bud, with a thickened stem section and modified leaves (daffodil). Clear as mud, right?

Most flowering bulbs need plenty of sunlight, at least when their foliage is out, which means many spring bulbs get all the sun they need even when planted under summer-shady oaks and tall deciduous shrubs since the trees still haven't leafed out by late winter and early spring. Be careful, however, to avoid planting them in the shadow of the north side of a building or evergreen shrubs, because the combination of the winter and early spring sun being so low in the southern sky and the dim setting will mean that the bulbs won't get enough light.

Bulbs also usually require well-drained soil and certainly shouldn't be planted where water stands for hours after a rain. Avoid water-related bulb rot by working plenty of organic matter or coarse sand into heavy soils, or plant in raised beds or containers.

Garden centers, mail-order catalogues, and specialty nurseries have many dozens of different kinds of bulbs, each with several distinct species and sometimes hundreds of unique cultivars. It's always a great idea to try new kinds—you never know when one will turn out to be an all-time favorite in your garden. But for long-term success, see if there aren't enough different kinds of bulbs described here to keep you entertained for many years with little effort.

The planting rule of thumb for true bulbs, unless otherwise indicated, is "twice as deep as they are tall." Big bulbs go deeper than smaller ones. You can even plant smaller ones above larger ones!

Interplanting with Bulbs

Some bulbs bloom in early spring and are dormant in the summer; some perennials flower in the summer and are completely bare in the winter. Why waste precious garden space for "one shot" plants, when you can plant one in between the other to prolong the season? Bonus: The emerging foliage of one can hide the fading leaves of the other. Large shrubs, groundcovers, and overstuffed patio pots can all be gussied up with bulbs.

The biggest considerations for interplanting flowers include making sure that all of them get the amount of sun or shade they need, that watering or fertilizing one type doesn't harm the others, and of course planting larger ones where they won't hide smaller kinds.

Bulbs for the Shade

Ever see bulbs growing in old home places that are all grown up with trees? These "naturalized" beauties have spread by seed, because their fruiting pods were left intact instead of being mowed or clipped before their seed ripened.

The trick to getting them to grow and multiply in the shade is planting them under trees which lose their leaves in the winter, giving them winter sunshine, and leaving them alone after flowering so they have time to form next year's flower buds underground inside the bulbs.

The bottom line is, plant bulbs, especially early-flowering kinds, where they get winter sunshine, and then leave them alone after they flower. And don't cut their foliage while green! Wait until the leaves have yellowed at least two-thirds of the way down, meaning they are almost finished storing all the food the bulbs will need for the big show next season.

TIP: Bulb foods are best for bulbs. They need a balanced fertilizer containing nitrogen, phosphorous, and potash, in small amounts. Bone meal alone has only phosphorous, just one of the main ingredients needed for overall plant health and growth. Of course the best bulbs are the ones that don't require special fertilizers. But use bulb food if you want; it is specially formulated for that type of plant. Though an occasional feeding with all-purpose fertilizer is also fine.

Tulips Hate California

Tulips are annuals in California, period. Many daffodils are as well. Showy and nostalgic as they are, they're best used for one-shot foliage and spring flowers—like equally beautiful (and intensely fragrant) hybrid hyacinths. They are native perennials in areas that have cold winters and dry summers—because of California's mild winters they usually don't get the "chilling hours" they need to rebloom or they simply rot from wet springs or irrigation. Plus, the new bulbs they produce take energy from the "mother" bulbs while requiring a couple or more years to get to blooming size, and everything just peters out.

Sure, you could dig and clean and store them, and refrigerate them before planting again, but c'mon—what's the point? Buy a cheap sackful every fall, refrigerate them for five or six weeks before planting, then stick them in groups here and there where you want winter texture and spring flowers. Then feed them to the compost.

Try early-flowering species tulips (*Tulipa bakeri, T. clusiana, T. clusiana* var. *chrysantha, T. saxatilis, T. sylvestris, T. tarda*), and paper-white daffodils (*Narcissus tazetta*), planted in raised beds or pots for good drainage.

Protect Bulbs from Critters

Naked Ladies

Who hasn't endured the bulb-eating onslaught of gophers or chipmunks? Not much will control these destructive pests—they are even hard for cats to catch!

Here are some "tricks of the trade" used by hard-core gardeners, and in botanical gardens:

- When planting bulbs, surround them with gravel or other coarse material, which critters hate digging through.
- For squirrels, place "live" traps near burrows, baited with something smeared with peanut butter.
- When digging beds, place hardware cloth (mesh wire with $1/2$-inch openings) in the bottom and up the sides, like an upside-down fence. Cut a trench around the beds and line it with the strip of hardware cloth at least 6 or 8 inches tall, partly sticking out of the ground (mulch will cover the exposed part). Make sure the bottom edge is curved outward, away from the bed, to guide pests away, not under.
- Plant individual bulbs or plants in wire baskets buried partially in the ground.
- Protect from digging tree squirrels, chipmunks, and cats by laying "chicken wire" over the planted area, which bulbs will grow up through.

Move Bulbs When Dormant

Got a friend or neighbor who has bulbs you want, or know an old home place that is about to be developed and you have permission to get a few? Take your time—don't rush out to dig when plants are in full bloom, for two reasons: Digging when in flower often causes them to skip a year blooming (which means it will be two years until the next flowering cycle), and someone you know will invariably come down the road just as you get back to your car with an armload and wonder what you're up to! Mark the plants you want with a discreet marker, like a plastic knife, then come back when the bulbs are going dormant to dig a few for your own garden.

Autumn Crocus
Colchicum species
Sun or light shade

If late summer surprises are your thing, these usually pink flowers (which are not true crocus) will do the trick, as they arise without foliage when most other bulbs are still dormant, blooming even into fall. Fantastic in well-drained rock gardens or naturalized on lightly wooded slopes, these hardy corms can be left undisturbed for many years.

FLOWER: Tight clusters of 3-inch-wide pink, rose-purple, or white flowers flare open atop slender stems, with outer flowers sometimes flopping under their own weight.

PLANT: Thick-scaled corms send up broad leaves up to a foot long in the spring and should be kept only barely moist when dormant.

INTERESTING KINDS: Single lavender 'The Giant' hybrid is most readily available but look for double, violet 'Waterlily'.

Belladonna Lily or Naked Ladies
Amaryllis belladonna
Winter sun

This most beloved old-time garden plant—said to outlive the gardeners who plant them—can still be found marking abandoned homesteads across California, with large flowers emerging from bare ground. It gets all the water it needs from even sparse winter rains.

FLOWER: Leafless stalks in mid- to late summer are topped with several large, fragrant, trumpets of pink or rose.

PLANT: Readily multiplying, fist-size bulbs produce bold, strap-like leaves in the fall and winter, which wither by late spring. Requires no maintenance other than occasional dividing for sharing.

INTERESTING KINDS: The later-blooming hybrid 'Amarygia' (a named coined by Les Hannibal, a breeder from Sacramento) comes in pure white, delicate pinks, and near-reds, often with contrasting white centers.

Canna

Canna × generalis

Sun or very light shade

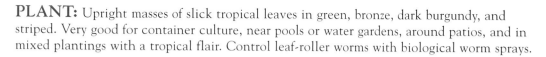

This old Victorian garden mainstay is still one of the most widely summer-planted beauties, grown by upscale horticulturists and rural gardeners alike for bold foliage and flowers. Loves heat and extra water.

FLOWER: Sometimes very showy, gnarly masses of irregularly shaped flowers in orange, red, yellow, apricot, salmon, and mixed.

PLANT: Upright masses of slick tropical leaves in green, bronze, dark burgundy, and striped. Very good for container culture, near pools or water gardens, around patios, and in mixed plantings with a tropical flair. Control leaf-roller worms with biological worm sprays.

INTERESTING KINDS: Too many to list, but look for 'Bengal Tiger' with bright yellow stripes, maroon margins, and orange flowers; 'Tropicanna' with shocking stripes of red, pink, and orange; and red-foliaged 'Wyoming'.

Crinum

Crinum species

Sun, light shade in hot areas

Though sometimes hard to locate commercially, this large, bold bulb is sturdy beyond compare—it is said that none have ever died! I once photographed one growing in broken glass between the sidewalk and curb beside a beer joint.

FLOWER: Stalks up to 4 feet tall topped with nodding clusters of slender trumpets up to a foot long, either white, pink, wine-red, or white with reddish stripes.

PLANT: Floppy eruptions of long, wide, strap-like leaves remain in large clumps for many years. May go winter-dormant in colder areas of California. Tips of new growth sometimes get caught in the twisted dried remains of previous year's foliage.

INTERESTING KINDS: If you can find a good supplier, look for nearly red 'Ellen Bosanquet', pink ruffled 'Emma Jones', pink with white streaks 'Carnival'. Others have burgundy foliage.

Crocosmia

Crocosmia species

Sun or light shade

An excellent airy flower for adding a touch of color with other summer perennials, this foolproof old garden mainstay is perfect both for beginners and more skillful designers and flower arrangers who want lots for very little effort.

FLOWER: Related to freesia, the wiry branched stems arch under the weight of 1- to 2-inch-wide orange, red, yellow, or cream flowers that open continually for weeks. Excellent as cut flowers.

PLANT: Spreading clumps with sword-like leaves up to 3 feet tall, some can naturalize to the point of weediness.

INTERESTING KINDS: Old-fashioned orange montbretia (C. × *crocosmiiflora*) is invasive; hybrid 'Citronella' is compact with yellow flowers and a dark eye; 'Lucifer' has bright red flowers; 'Jenny Bloom' is yellow; 'Solfatare' has bronze foliage and yellow flowers.

Crocus

Crocus species

Sun

This low-flowering bulb naturalizes well in rock gardens, between stepping stones, and in the lawn.

FLOWER: Small, narrow chalices in a wide range of colors appear, depending on variety, in fall, winter, or spring. Stems are below ground, creating a flower carpet effect.

PLANT: Clumps of grass-like leaves, may have a pale midrib stripe. Won't spread readily in warm-winter areas.

INTERESTING KINDS: Fall-blooming saffron crocus (C. *sativus*) has lilac flowers whose pollen-bearing stigmas are clipped off and used as seasoning (use pollen from a dozen flowers per dish); C. *imperati* is a dependable early-spring purplish species; C. *goulimyi*, another fall bloomer, bears sweetly scented, clear lavender flowers.

Daffodils
Narcissus species
Sun or light shade

My earliest childhood memories are very fragrant paper-whites with multiple white flowers on each stem, and skinny yellow jonquils with their heady bouquet. Narcissus is Latin for "daffodil"—species and varieties aside, they are one and the same, and they come in a wide array of flower forms and fragrances, and some varieties (though not all) multiply rapidly year after year in California.

FLOWER: Varies with the species. Stalks from 6 inches to over 2 feet tall produce single blooms or clusters of six-petalled flowers, usually with an elongated cup in the center. Double forms, large-cup, short-cup, split corona (cup looks like it has extra petals), in white, yellow, gold, pink, orange, and many combinations.

PLANT: Butter-knife-like leaves arise in clumps in late fall or winter, and die down after flowering is finished in the spring (very important to allow foliage to yellow naturally before cutting). *Narcissus jonquilla* has distinct, reedy foliage similar to porcupine quills. Bulbs are toxic, so chipmunks, gophers, and voles leave them alone.

INTERESTING KINDS: Though there are hundreds of great daffodils to try, these have proven themselves to be long-lived and prolific bloomers in California: 'Bridal Crown', double flowered, pure white; 'Carlton', large cupped soft yellow; 'Cheerfulness', white double tazetta; 'Erlicheer', very fragrant, small double white flowers in clusters; 'February Gold', golden yellow trumpet with pale yellow swept-back petals; 'Geranium', white and orange; 'Mount Hood', large trumpet, white; 'Silver Chimes', several creamy white fragrant flowers per stem; 'Thalia', white, two to three flowers per stem; 'Trevithian', bright yellow, two to three flowers per stem, very fragrant; 'Yellow Cheerfulness', creamy yellow; 'Accent', large pink cup, white petals; 'Hawera', soft yellow, recurved petals; 'Suzy', small red cups, ruffled yellow petals.

Why Daffodils Don't Bloom:

- Too much shade on foliage.
- Poor drainage or heavy irrigation rots bulbs.
- Too much nitrogen fertilizer or no fertilizer at all.
- Crowded bulbs may need lifting and dividing.
- Leaves were cut off too early in the spring.
- Plants moved when in flower.
- Variety not suited for California.

51

Dahlia
Dahlia hybrids
Sun or part sun

Native to Mexico and Guatemala, this summer-loving plant has spectacular blooms, from the small bedding types set out in borders as annuals, to the obscenely large cut-flower dinnerplate-size kinds.

FLOWER: Many-petalled daisy-like flowers from 2 to 12 inches across, can be single, double, balled, pompom, cactus, and other shapes, in every color but true blue. Large flowering kinds are excellent cut flowers.

PLANT: Summer-growing, with both short compact varieties and tall kinds that require staking, with leaves divided into many large, deep green or burgundy leaflets. Requires well-drained soil, so plant in raised beds or large containers.

INTERESTING KINDS: Multi-stemmed tree dahlia (*D. imperialis*) can grow well over 10 feet tall with daisy like flowers up to 8 inches across.

Dutch Iris
Iris hybrids
Sun

Unlike the commonly planted, thick-rooted rhizome-type iris, this is a true bulb that tolerates winter cold or summer heat—but not a lot of summer irrigation—and makes an excellent cut flower.

FLOWER: Small iris flowers of white, blue, purple, orange, yellow, and bicolor combinations carried on slender stems in the late winter or early spring.

PLANTS: Round bulbs can be left in the ground for many years in places where they won't rot from excessive summer watering. The foliage is narrow and rush-like, and dies down quickly after flowers fade.

INTERESTING KINDS: Very widely sold 'Wedgewood' has early-blooming, large lavender-blue flowers with yellow markings; many others are available every fall, very inexpensive and easy to stick in the ground between other perennials.

Flowering Onion
Allium species
Sun

There are many species of these unusual flowering bulbs ("regular" onions and garlic are also *Allium*), which have single stems topped with roundish flowers that are often used as cut flowers. Some are sweetly fragrant (those that smell like onions have to be bruised to give off their odor).

FLOWER: Many thin individual flowers arranged in a globe or loose cluster atop leafless stems, from spring through summer. Colors range from white to yellow, pink, reddish, lavender, blue, or purple.

PLANT: Clump-forming bulbs with spiked leaves that are either cylidrical and hollow, or flattened and swordlike, ranging from a few inches to over 2 feet tall.

INTERESTING KINDS: Drumsticks allium (*A. sphaerocephalon*) has tight red-purple clusters, and spreads readily; 'Grandiflorum' (*A. neopolitanum*) has large white flowers and is grown as a cut flower; garlic (*A. sativum*) and the giant elephant garlic (*A. scorodoprasum*) are as ornamental as they are edible.

Gladiolus
Gladiolus species and hybrids
Sun

Gladiolus is the ultimate summer cut flower. Just stick a handful of corms into the ground, add stakes to keep the tall plants from falling over, and stand back! Plant in batches over a period of time for a continuous show.

FLOWER: Narrow, 3- to 4-foot spikes of showy flaring flowers that open a few at a time all on the same side of the stem, from the bottom up. Outstanding cut flower in red, yellow, orange, apricot, white, purple, and many combinations.

PLANT: Upright fan of sword-like leaves grows from an inexpensive corm.

INTERESTING KINDS: Many "grandiflora" hybrids. *Gladiolus tristis* is a small, tough species commonly available, with fragrant, yellowish flowers with purple veins. Hardy gladiolus (*G. communis* ssp. *byzantinus*) is an old-garden variety with bright magenta flowers.

Grape Hyacinth
Muscari species
Sun

This prolific, self-seeding little Mediterranean native produces an early-spring haze of blue; great for naturalizing in lawns, or tucked into rock gardens.

FLOWER: Small, light- to dark-blue or white urn-shaped bells packed and scented like grapes on 6- to 10-inch stems.

PLANT: Short clumps of thin, grasslike leaves from fall to spring. One of the earliest bulbs to send up foliage, it can get so thick it nearly chokes itself out.

INTERESTING KINDS: *Muscari armeniacum* 'Blue Spike' has double flowers of pale blue; *M. latifolium* has much larger flowers than the old-timey grape hyacinth and is better suited for mixed-flower borders where it's less likely to get lost under other plants. *Muscari comosum* has pinkish-purple feathery flowers.

Hardy Cyclamen
Cyclamen species
Sun or light shade

Beyond the showy but tender florist cyclamen (*C. persicum*), hardy outdoor species, all of which can also be grown in pots, are very durable rock garden or shade groundcovers that can spread by seed into areas even under shrubs and native oaks.

FLOWER: Floppy, butterfly-like on short stems above foliage, in white, pink, rose, lavender, and crimson.

PLANT: Attractive small mounds of roundish or heart-shaped leaves, often mottled with pale green, gray, silver or white. Most go dormant in midsummer.

INTERESTING KINDS: One of the hardiest and most vigorous for outdoor culture is Neapolitan cyclamen (*C. hederifolium*) with large green leaves marbled with white or silver. *Cyclamen coum* usually has crimson rose flowers in winter and early spring.

Nerine

Nerine species

Sun or very light shade

Very similar to "spider lily" (*Lycoris*), these airy bloomers always surprise and delight with their sudden appearance from seemingly bare ground.

FLOWER: Red, yellow, gold, or pink flowers with narrow petals are clustered atop leafless stems up to 2 feet tall, appearing in late summer while foliage is dormant.

PLANT: Tight clumps of narrow leaves to a foot long appear in the fall and usually die back by early summer, though some forms hold old foliage until new appears. Can spread rapidly.

INTERESTING KINDS: Guernsey lily (*N. sarniensis*) is a sturdy old species most commonly found with large clusters of crimson flowers. *Nerine bowdenii* has several forms. *Nerine crispa* is 1 foot tall with pale pink flowers. There are other taller kinds with crimson or red flowers.

Painted Arum

Arum italicum

Winter sun

This surprising winter-foliage and spring-flowering heirloom, most often found in old established gardens where people have swapped plants, fills a huge gap left where summer perennials have gone dormant for the winter.

FLOWER: Foot-tall spike is topped with a sail-like spathe that encloses a finger-like spadix. Blossoms are followed by a stalk covered with showy red berry-like fruits.

PLANT: Very showy arrowhead-shaped leaves to a foot or more tall appear in the fall and winter and go dormant in the summer. Invasive, but in a good way.

INTERESTING KINDS: 'Pictum' has very showy white-veined leaves. Black calla (*A. pictum*) has a violet spathe with a white base and purple spadix. Spathes of *A. palaestinum* are green on the outside, purple inside with a black spadix.

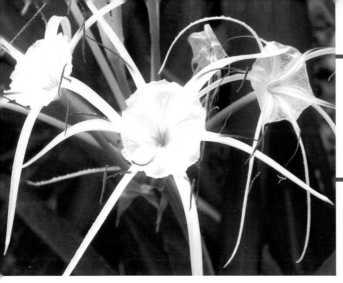

Peruvian Daffodil
Hymenocallis species
Sun

This one likes it *hot*! Looking for all the world like a cross between a naked lady (belladonna lily, p. 48) and a daffodil, this summer-bloomer is hardy in all but the coldest mountain areas.

FLOWER: Spidery petals, sometimes slightly curly, extend beyond a broad cup atop sturdy stems. Usually green-striped but can be white or yellow. Fragrant.

PLANT: Strap-like leaves up to 2 feet tall can last all summer if kept watered.

INTERESTING KINDS: Basket flower (*H. narcissiflora*, most commonly called Peruvian daffodil) has green-striped flowers. 'Advance' is pure white with a very faint green throat; 'Sulfur Queen' is less spidery, soft yellow with green stripes in the throat.

Snowflake
Leucojum aestivum
Winter sun

Sometimes called summer snowflake, or erroneously snowdrops (the common name for another, similar bulb, *Galanthus nivalis*) don't let the name fool you, this heirloom spring bloomer is one of the toughest bulbs for naturalizing—it often spreads from old homesteads into shrub borders, orchards, and even ditch banks.

FLOWER: Nodding, bell-shaped blooms, usually three to five per stem, are white with a distinct green dot on each petal.

PLANT: Foliage looks exactly like that of daffodils. Bulbs multiply very readily. Flowers best when crowded or undisturbed.

INTERESTING KINDS: 'Gravetye Giant' has up to nine flowers per stem and is a little taller than the species. Spring snowflake (*L. vernum*) has only one or two flowers per stem, and requires cold winters to thrive.

Spanish Bluebells
Hyacinthoides hispanica
Winter sun

Sometimes still sold as *Scilla campanulata*, this spiky old pioneer favorite (once called *Endymion* or "woods hyacinth") looks like a loose hyacinth, without the fragrance. It can spread and reseed readily, and often outlives the gardener who plants it!

FLOWER: Strongly upright stems up to 18 inches tall hold a dozen or more well-spaced blue (sometimes pink or white) bells, each over half an inch long.

PLANT: Stiff, deep green foliage remains upright until nearly dormant in the late winter. Very prolific spreader; can be divided repeatedly. Grows well under deciduous trees and shrubs and tolerates both moist and dry soils.

INTERESTING KINDS: The most commonly grown form is 'Excelsior' with deep blue flowers.

Starflower
Ipheion uniflorum
Winter sun

One of mid-winter's low-growing fragrant delights, this small old-fashioned bulb can persist for decades, multiplying and spreading under trees and into the lawn, creating a starry carpet of pale blue. By late spring it is completely dormant, but persists even in dry soil filled with tree roots.

FLOWER: Dozens of quarter-size pale blue stars streaked with lighter blue, held just above the foliage from late January through early March. Violet-like fragrance.

PLANT: Pale green, grass-like clumps up to about 6 inches high, early to come up in the fall and early to go down in the spring.

INTERESTING KINDS: 'Wisley Blue' is a commonly available, bright blue selection. 'Album' has white flowers and 'Froyle Mill' has violet flowers.

Tuberose

Polianthes tuberosa

Sun or light shade

A Mexican native noted for its powerfully sweet, gardenia-like fragrance, this summer- and fall-flowering plant is an old-time garden favorite, dating back to the days before deodorants and room fresheners.

FLOWER: Pure white tubes are loosely arranged in clusters near the tops of 3-foot spikes.

PLANT: Bulb-like rhizomes spread fairly well into clumps of grassy foliage. Often dug and stored over the winter, but can be left in the ground for many years; will quickly rot in poorly-drained or over-watered soils. Suitable for growing in containers that are allowed to dry out in the winter.

INTERESTING KINDS: 'Mexican Single' is the best cut flower; 'The Pearl' is a popular double-flowering form. 'Marginata' has white-edged leaves.

Voodoo Lily

Amorphophallus bulbifer

Part shade, shade

No doubt one of the creepiest plants for California gardens, this woodland or shade plant, though sometimes hard to find commercially, is sure to get gasps of attention from visitors.

FLOWER: Fleshy, light burgundy stalk with purple spots to 3 feet tall, with the top half of the spike being a slightly unwrapped hood-like bract, with the aroma of rotten meat for attracting pollinating flies.

PLANT: Fat bulb-like tuber shoots up a single 3- to 4-foot fleshy stalk topped with a wide, deeply-divided, umbrella-like leaf.

INTERESTING KINDS: Flower stalk and leaf stalk of *A. konjac* get up to 6 feet tall; *A. paeonifolius* gets even larger with a wide, ruffled purple-and-green spathe spotted with white. The most commonly grown voodoo lily planted in California is sold as *Drancunculus vulgaris*.

WHILE "FORCING" BULBS TO BLOOM INDOORS ISN'T EXACTLY A "TOUGH PLANTS" PRACTICE, perhaps the easiest are inexpensive paper-white narcissus. They don't require as much cooling to flower. Simply put a few in a small pot, fill around them with gravel to keep them upright, and fill halfway up the bulbs with water. Keep in a cool place indoors until they start growing; then move them to a sunny window and keep them watered. Note: After being forced in water, these bulbs are completely shot and will not rebloom. Compost them.

Other Good Bulbs:

These may not be as easy, or as dependable, but are tempting enough to try—at least for awhile:

Amaryllis (*Hippeastrum* hybrids) has bold flowers and bold foliage. It goes dormant, and requires watering to keep it going for years. Most gardeners keep them potted, let them go dormant for a few months, then start watering again.

Blazing Star (*Liatris* species) is native to the eastern U.S., and has grasslike foliage and tall spires of lavender-purple flowers that bloom from the top down so florists can clip the tips off as the flowers fade.

Caladium (*Caladium bicolor*), one of the boldest-foliage annuals, is hard to grow well without shade and water—and still can have leaf-burn if allowed to dry, or rot if overwatered. Best for containers, and fed regularly.

Freesia (*Freesia* hybrids) is easy, prolific, and elegant—but subject to freezing, and hates heat, wind, and drought. 'Nuff said.

Persian Buttercup (*Ranunculus asiaticus*)—see Freesia.

(For more information on bulbs, their planting and care, look for the *California Gardener's Guide*, published by Cool Springs Press.)

 Best for Beginners:

- *Autumn Crocus*
- *Belladonna Lily*
- *Canna*
- *Crocosmia*
- *Gladiolus*
- *Grape Hyacinth*
- *Snowflake*

Kinda Tricky:

- *Dahlia*
- *Flowering Onion*
- *Iris*
- *Tuberose*
- *Voodoo Lily*

Amaryllis

Quintessence in the Garden

Ever find something that is so simple it can't be improved upon? There's a word for "just right" stuff: quintessence.

It usually does only one thing, but does it so well it would be hard to replace. Think hand-held pencil sharpener. A spatula can be used for shooing a lizard back outside, but it's mostly f or hot skillet stuff—hard to cook without one. Others would be smoke alarm, vacuum cleaner, hair brush, coffee filter, toilet plunger, TV remote control, and the mouse on my computer. We could get along without opposable thumbs, but they'd be sorely missed.

There is also quintessence in the garden: wheelbarrows, night lighting, leaf blowers, and other labor-saving tools taken for granted. Some are multi-purpose, from five-gallon buckets and red wagons to balls of twine and chicken wire; often they have no moving parts, other than the gardener.

Then there is the little stuff that falls somewhere between necessary and just plain handy, like crunchy perlite that does nothing but lighten potting soils. Some we really don't need, but they do a job well while working on the simplest level. Ideal tools which embody the principles of simplicity and rightness include garden hose, watering can, hose-end water valve, leaf rake, pincushion sprinkler, flat metal file, self-locking plastic cable ties, and, for flower arrangers, a metal "frog" or green oasis blocks.

Garden accessories that go to the heart of gardening without adding clutter to our lives include hummingbird feeder, wind chimes, rain gauge, outdoor thermometer, weather vane, tiki torch, and porch swing.

Some living things carry the simple essence of gardening spirit. My short list would include gourds, shade trees, seeds, hot peppers, rosemary, and such universally grown flowers as California poppies, jade plant, and old roses. And the dogface butterfly, California's official state butterfly.

These are a mere smattering of "just right, almost can't garden without" items that do only one thing, but do it so well they'd be hard to garden without. In other words, they're quintessential!

Grasses
WITH GUMPTION

Ornamental grasses bring the landscape to life! Shrub-like and groundcover grasses have been grown in California botanical and cottage gardens for many decades—in fact, the American Bamboo Society was started in 1979 at Quail Botanical Garden in Encinitas, which has the largest bamboo collection in the United States and serves as a USDA quarantine site for new introductions.

Yet other than the common use of bamboo and giant reed—and the notorious garden escape act performed by pampas grass—only in the past couple of decades have grasses become more widely accepted as very tough "foils" for other landscape plants. Now they are being used even around fast-food restaurants!

In addition to the other senses, their visual effect is of color, richness, and texture. They come in a wide variety of shapes, colors, variegations, and long-stemmed flowers that are long lasting in both fresh and dried cut-flower arrangements. Some grasses grow in tight clumps; others "run" or spread. The plants can be used as specimens, in groups, as a groundcover, in naturalistic masses, and even in containers.

While some prefer shade and a few tolerate moist soils (though some even grow in water gardens), most grow best in sunny, dry locations. They put out new growth in the spring, flower in the summer and fall, and have no major

Blue Lyme Grass

 **Best for Beginners:**

- *Blue Fescue*
- *Clump-Forming Bamboos*
- *Fountain Grass*
- *Miscanthus*
- *River Oats*

Kinda Tricky:

- *Horsetail*
- *Japanese Blood Grass*
- *Running Bamboos*

Bamboo

pests. Most gardeners leave the foliage alone, but some cut the old growth back in the late winter to help new growth come out clean and fresh; be sure to do this before new growth begins to come up, or it may look ragged all summer.

On the following pages are super-hardy grasses that have been commonly grown for many decades by California gardeners.

BAMBOO IS NOT THE THUG THAT MANY PEOPLE THINK IT IS. Most gardeners who have problems with bamboo have the "running" kind, especially members of the *Phyllostachys* genus that includes "fishing pole" bamboo, giant timber bamboo, the beautiful black bamboo, and others. These very cold-hardy bamboos have almost woody underground stems that can shoot in any direction and, when cut, can send new plants up at every joint. They can take over entire landscapes—and the gardens of neighbors, too! Running bamboos can be contained—at least for a while—with trenches, foot-deep edging, and a little luck. Otherwise, herbicides will have to be brought in.

On the other hand, some very beautiful kinds of bamboos stay in slow-to-spread clumps. Quite a few are in the *Bambusa* genus, which includes some that get very tall but take many years to spread even a few feet.

Black Bamboo

Black Bamboo (*Phyllostachys nigra*) is a "running" type bamboo, one of many great ones that include golden or variegated kinds, giant timber types, and dozens of others. Black bamboo has chocolate-brown stems and narrow leaves, and looks fantastic when grown against a solid wall backdrop.

Blue Fescue (*Festuca glauca* 'Elijah Blue' and 'Siskiyou Blue') is a dense, foot or more tall clump of blue gray with airy summer flower spikes. Used as a border plant, specimen, or a ground stabilizer. California fescue (*F. californica* 'Serpentine Blue') is a native with purple or deep yellow flower spikes; native Idaho blue fescue (*F. idahoensis*) is perhaps the best of the lot, tolerating more wet winter and being less likely to die out in the center. Blue oat grass (*Helictotrichon sempervirens*) is similar to blue fescue, but is larger and more graceful and can be evergreen (everblue?) in mild-winter areas.

Blue Fescue

Blue Lyme Grass

Blue Lyme Grass (*Leymus arenarius*) is a low clumping grass with striking blue-gray leaves that spreads slowly but steadily. 'Findhorn' is a compact variety good for small areas. *Leymus condensatus* 'Canyon Blue' is a coastal and Channel Island native that starts out greenish and matures to brilliant silvery blue.

Clumping Bamboo (*Bambusa multiplex*) is a group of generally tall, clump-forming or slow-to-spread grasses with narrow leaves produced in joints of tall, hollow, woody canes. 'Golden Goddess' is not very thick but is tall and bushy, making it a good screen plant.

Clumping Bamboo

Dwarf Bamboo

Dwarf Bamboo (*Pleioblastus pygmaeus* or *Arundinaria pygmaea*) is a ground-cover bamboo to 3 feet tall, very thick and aggressive even in dense shade. Must be contained by walks or deep metal or plastic edging.

Giant Feather Grass

Giant Feather Grass (*Stipa gigantea*) forms a clump of narrow, arching leaves to 3 feet tall, with a broad cloud of yellowish flowers 3 feet above the foliage.

Japanese Blood Grass

Japanese Blood Grass (*Imperata cylindrica* 'Red Baron') features upright clumps to 2 feet tall with the upper portions of foliage a rich, almost blood-red. Though a cultivar of the very invasive "cogon" grass (the species *I. cylindrica*), this striking cultivar spreads slowly and rarely flowers.

Lemon Grass (*Cymbopogon citratus*) is a waist-high grass that has a strong citrus aroma in its leaves and stems. Used as a culinary herb or just to make the garden smell a little zesty. It grows well in raised beds and containers, but may freeze in cold-winter areas, so be prepared to bring a piece of it indoors.

Lemon Grass

Maiden Grass (*Miscanthus sinensis*) is a versatile clump-forming fountain-like grass with narrow flowering stems topped with curly, feathery plumes that last well into the winter. Interesting cultivars include bold 'Cosmopolitan', slender 'Gracillimus', cross-striped 'Strictus' (creamy stripes that run across the leaves), and compact 'Yaku Jima' and 'Adagio'. Evergreen miscanthus (*M. transmorrisonensis*) can remain green all year in warm areas.

Maiden Grass

Mexican Feather Grass (*Stipa tenuissima*) is one of several native "needle" grasses with very fine texture and a very showy billowy effect. It is fairly weedy but can be controlled with a little effort.

Mexican Feather Grass

Purple Fountain Grass

Purple Fountain Grass (*Pennisetum setaceum* 'Rubrum') is not a self-seeding invasive like its common green cousin, though it can live practically in gravel. The upright clump has reddish purple leaves and rosy-burgundy plumes right up until winter, when it turns brown (even in mild areas). Showy as a specimen in a container or by a gate, it is spectacular when mass-planted in a street boulevard. The 'Burgundy Giant' cultivar gets up to 5 feet tall.

Purple Muhly Grass

Purple Muhly Grass (*Muhlenbergia capillaris*) is an outstanding knee-high clump of slender foliage, not much to look at until late summer when it's covered with airy, billowy masses of striking pinkish-red flowers. Other good muhly grasses include blue Mexican muhly (M. *pubescens*), and deer grass (M. *rigens*). Bamboo muhly (hair grass, M. *dumosa*) is a billowy, light green clump up to 7 feet tall, looking like a very fine, non-spreading bamboo.

Ribbon Grass (*Phalaris arundinacea*) is a very aggressive creeping groundcover to 2 or more feet high, an excellent border plant or "skirt" for shrubbery even in shaded areas. It ought to be contained or it will get out of control. Turns brown at first frost in cold areas of the state. 'Picta' has white-striped leaves.

Ribbon Grass

Switch Grass

Switch Grass (*Panicum virgatum*) is a native prairie bunch grass with narrow leaves. Summer blooms rise above the foliage up to 5 or 6 feet or more, opening into pinkish clouds that fade to white. Foliage has good yellow fall color except in the mild-winter areas. Sways and dances with coastal winds.

River Oats (*Chasmanthium latifolium*) is a Southeastern riverbank native for full sun or moderate shade, with stiff, knee-high, narrow-wiry, bamboo-like stems. Topped with numerous arching flower stalks with two dozen or more dangling florets that have been compared to little fish or even "flattened armadillos." The stems hold up very well in dried arrangements.

River Oats

Invasive Grasses:

Even though some of these are recommended in this chapter as easy and tough, they are best if contained or grown in a pot (or avoided):

- **Fountain Grass** (*Pennisetum setaceum*)—invasive list

- **Pampas Grass** (*Cortaderia selloana*)—invasive list

- **Striped Cane** (*Arundo donax* 'Variegata')—invasive list

- **Dwarf Bamboo** (*Pleioblastus pygmaeus* or *Arundinaria pygmaea*)

- **Ribbon Grass** (*Phalaris arundinacea*)

- **Mexican Feather Grass** (*Stipa tenuissima*)

- **Running Bamboo** (*Phyllostachys* species)

- **Blue Lyme Grass** (*Leymus arenarius*)

Ribbon Grass

EVEN ORNAMENTAL GRASSES NEED MOWING, AT LEAST IF YOU WANT TO KEEP THEM NEAT. There's no "absolute need" to do this, other than for cosmetic purposes—if you don't prune the old growth, new foliage will cover it up by late spring. Once a year, in mid- to late winter, give the old foliage a neat shearing so the new spring growth will come out nice and clean. And, tempting as it may be, of course *don't set fire to them* or risk killing the center of the clump, not to mention losing your eyebrows and sending the entire town up in blazes! Approach grasses from an angle with sharp shears or a fast-running string trimmer, going around and around like eating an ice cream cone, gradually getting down to the main clump.

Feng Shui Isn't a Nasty Word

Feng shui (pronounced fung-shway) is the coupling of common sense and the art of good placement to create a pleasing relationship between us, our home, and environment. It includes the balanced use of spaces, views, energies, materials, textures, and experiences.

Feng shui (which means the flow of "wind" and "water") tries to minimize that which is bad, and put to use that which is good, with a balance of contrasts ("yin" and "yang"). Without getting into detail, and knowing that no two gardeners do anything alike, here are just a few elements of "good" feng shui design for the garden:

Doors and gates should be attractive, neat, welcoming; paving should be comfortably wide and inviting. Straight lines, including front walks, and pointed objects should be toned down or partially hidden with plants; vines can soften walls and cover sharp edges. Naturalistic pruning techniques lower maintenance and keep things from being too contrived.

Landscaping should take advantage of natural energy. Trees, arbors, vines, and awnings provide summer shade yet block chilly winds, and allow winter sun to warm the home and garden. A water feature with movement, preferably across the view, not away from the house, can be soothing; lights or mirrors can brighten dark corners; overgrown shrubs can be "limbed up" to encourage air movement.

Sizes, shapes, textures, and harmonious colors of plants should be varied, and other elements balanced; create areas of light and shade, open and hidden views, water with rocks, wood with metal, etc. Statues, rocks, and other accessories including benches, trellises, a fish pond, and sounds (wind chimes) should be in scale with the rest of the garden (no miniature windmills, no oversized naked goddess statues), and not overdone.

Finally, there should be butterflies, birds, movement, gentle sounds. Any small steps you take, physically or by creating perceptions, to foster a mood of balance and calm in your garden, brings security and peace, which is a large part of being happy. And that's just good feng shui.

Groundcovers
WITH GRIT

Ivy is not the only low-growing, spreading plant for the landscape—there are dozens of "ground covering" alternatives that not only look good all year but are incredibly low maintenance.

Ivy

Using groundcover plants has become one of the biggest trends in landscaping, a shift away from the wall-to-wall carpet of high maintenance turfgrass with its taskmaster demands on our precious time, water, energy, and pocketbooks, and its pest problems. In fact, almost everyone now recognizes that having a large percent of the landscape in turfgrass, besides being a huge environmental liability, is just not good design. Some university horticulturists are even calling those who over-water, over-feed, and over-spray lawns "environmental offenders." Strong words but basically on target.

In practical terms, there are many situations where turfgrass is simply not workable or sensible. In older neighborhoods with mature trees and large shrubs, grass has a hard time getting enough sunlight to continue reproducing itself and it gradually peters out or fades under the pressures of insects, diseases, or hard water. In many cases, large areas are impossible to mow or water frequently so drought-tolerant weeds take over and not only look bad but can actually become fire hazards later.

Groundcovers, much like a neat lawn area, can create a strong "unity" to the landscape by visually tying plants, buildings, and other elements together in a smooth visual flow. Depending on the type you plant, groundcovers can be used in the following ways:

- Will grow in densely shaded areas.
- Cover dry or sandy spots, even on salt-laden beach areas.
- Compete well with and hide surface tree roots.
- Fill in difficult to mow areas between shrubs, trees, and paved areas.
- Tolerate intense heat and sun in parking lot or boulevard strips.
- Add a cascading effect to large container plantings.
- Act as a foot-traffic barrier.
- Absorb rainfall run-off from buildings and paved areas, and lessen erosion.
- Provide interest with year-round foliage texture and seasonal flower color.

Depending on what kind of groundcover you choose, how it is planted, and how closely spaced new plants are, it may take a year or two, perhaps even longer, to get it to fill in completely enough to be relatively weed-free. An organic mulch such as shredded bark can help the appearance of a new groundcover area, plus it helps shade the soil to help groundcover roots get established quickly and conserve water, smothers many weed seeds, and feeds the soil as it decomposes. Note: Mulches applied too heavily may slow down new rooting of some groundcovers.

When buying or dividing groundcover plants, make sure they are well rooted. Some can be cut into smaller plants to make your groundcover dollars go farther. You also can plant a few one year and then gradually expand your plantings by dividing them the next year.

Water groundcovers as needed—a good soaking every few days is much better than frequent light sprinklings—and fertilize lightly, if and when needed, with an all-purpose fertilizer no more than once or twice a year.

Viva la Difference!

Jasmine has small, pointy, glossy green leaves. So do many popular shrubs. If you plant them together, they run together visually, so no one can tell where one stops and the other begins. It is best to mix up leaf shapes and colors for more contrast. Ivy geranium with its big leaves contrasts with finer-textured grasses, or with large, bold-textured tropical plants. Plant variegated groundcovers with solid-green shrubs, or vice-versa.

Asiatic Jasmine
Trachelospermum asiaticum
Sun or shade

One of the very best groundcovers for sun or shade this popular vine can be clipped into tight mats or allowed to flow irregularly. It covers quickly but may need routine clipping to keep it off sidewalks.

FLOWER: Small fragrant white flowers are usually hidden in the foliage.

PLANT: Thin but vigorous self-branching vine has many small, pointed, glossy green leaves. It is such a rapid grower that its edges have to be clipped regularly. Can climb shrubs or small trees. Roots readily in the summer.

INTERESTING KINDS: Only the species is widely available.

Beach Strawberry
Fragaria chiloensis
Sun or part shade

This California native is one of the "parents" of modern commercial strawberries but grown mostly for its matted foliage and white spring flowers.

FLOWER: Inch-wide white spring flowers are attractive enough. They are followed by very seedy red fruits in late summer.

PLANT: Three-leaflet leaves have toothed edges and can turn reddish in cool winters. Plants set a foot apart fill in with runners to become a thick mat under 6 inches high. Mow or cut in spring to remove old leaves and stems and encourage lush new growth.

INTERESTING KINDS: Alpine strawberry (*F. vesca*) does not produce runners and has small, fragrant, edible berries.

Bearberry Cotoneaster

Cotoneaster dammeri

Sun or light shade

Delicate foliage and bright red berries distinguish this tough, poor-soil-loving groundcover, which also grows well cascading from raised beds or containers.

FLOWER: Lots of small white or pinkish rose-like spring flowers. Bright red or orange-red berries last into the fall and winter, and are in greatest abundance when plants are grown on slopes or in other poor conditions—better than when grown in good garden soil.

PLANT: Spreading plant up to 8 to 10 feet wide, but remains a foot or less tall, with small, bright green leaves. Stems root where they touch the ground.

INTERESTING KINDS: 'Eichholz' remains under a foot tall and has a few orange-red berries in the fall; 'Coral Beauty' is only 6 inches tall; 'Lowfast' is a foot tall.

Carpet Bugle

Ajuga reptans

Shade or part shade

This very popular spreading groundcover for shade has many varieties and spreads almost too well.

FLOWER: Short spires rise above the mat of foliage with small but showy whorls of rich blue flowers in spring and early summer.

PLANT: Moderately spreading mass of creeping runners with oval leaves of deep green; leaves are more colorful with cultivars. Requires regular moisture, but can get root rot in poorly drained soils or where there is no air circulation. Plan on it escaping into the lawn, and dig all you can to share with friends.

INTERESTING KINDS: There are several good bronze-foliage selections, but for shade look for brighter variegated kinds such as 'Burgundy Lace' with reddish purple foliage tinged with pink and white, or 'Multicolor' with green, white, and pink variegation.

Creeping Juniper
Juniperus species
Sun or filtered sun

Among the toughest evergreens for sunny, harsh growing conditions including parking lot dividers, these salt- and drought-tolerant shrubs include many interesting species and cultivars. All grow well in any kind of soil, as long as it is well drained; they resent excessive irrigation.

FLOWER: Flowers go unnoticed, but shrubs can have blue berries in winter.

PLANT: Spreading evergreens with small, prickly green or blue-green needle-like leaves grow from under 6 inches to 2 feet high, and spread several feet in every direction. Some have plum or purple winter foliage.

INTERESTING KINDS: Shore (grows to 12 inches high), 'Prince of Wales' (8 inches), parson's (18 inches), blue rug (4 inches), dwarf Japanese garden (12 inches), 'Andorra' (2 feet), many others. Note: Tamarix juniper, commonly called TAM, is seriously overused considering how wide it grows and its unusually high level of pest problems.

Creeping Lilyturf
Liriope spicata
Shade or light shade

This dark green, grassy member of the lily family with its summer flower spikes will spread quickly in mulched, shady gardens. It "eats" fallen leaves under shrubs by catching the leaves on edge, making them compost more quickly.

FLOWER: Summer stalks of small, hyacinth-like, pinkish lavender flowers rarely rise above the foliage; blue-black berries persist into fall.

PLANT: Thick stands of narrow, evergreen grassy foliage a foot or so tall. Fast-spreading lilyturf has narrower leaves than the clump-forming *L. muscari*. If foliage looks ragged, cut or mow it in late winter before new growth emerges.

INTERESTING KINDS: 'Silver Dragon' is slower to spread than the species and has a silvery white stripe down the center of each leaf—a very nice touch in shaded areas.

Creeping Mahonia
Mahonia repens
Sun or shade

Though looking good all year, this low-spreading California woodland native is one of the best mahonias for fall colors.

FLOWER: Short clusters of yellow flowers in mid-spring are followed by blue berries.

PLANT: One foot tall and spreading in the winter by underground stems. The dull green summer foliage turns pinkish bronze in cool weather. Prune only to remove leggy or wayward old growth.

INTERESTING KINDS: Longleaf mahonia (M. *nervosa*) is a Northern California native that gets from 2 to 3 or so feet high and spreads by underground stems, with divided leaves up to 18 inches long that create the look of a stiff fern. This is an outstanding groundcover for dry shade.

Dwarf Periwinkle
Vinca minor
Light shade or shade

Unlike its thuggish larger cousin (V. *major*), which has become a serious garden escapee and has colonized large areas of California woodlands, this petite spreading species is tidier and more easily restrained.

FLOWER: Inch-wide, five-petal pinwheels of lavender blue, white, purple, or pink appear in late winter and spring along leaf joints.

PLANT: Creeping mass up to 6 inches high of thin branches and shiny dark green leaves about an inch or so long, spreading by runners. Can be sheared or mowed high after flowering to thicken the mat.

INTERESTING KINDS: 'Bowles' Variety' has larger leaves than the species and deep blue flowers; 'Ralph Shugert' has white-edged leaves and blooms again in the fall; V. *minor* f. *alba* has white flowers.

Ivy
Hedera helix
Sun or shade

Evergreen ivies have long been very popular groundcovers, in some cases completely replacing the need for grass in both sun and shade. Some are seriously invasive. However, not all ivies are alike, and even the hardiest kinds can behave differently in various settings.

'Ritterkreuz'

FLOWER: Mature plants have small white flowers and sometimes-showy black, yellow-orange, purple, or red berries edible to wildlife and viable enough to sprout miles from your garden.

PLANT: Rapidly-spreading, self-branching woody vine covered with deeply-lobed, ruffled, or smooth leaves that range from palmate (maple-like) to fan, shell, or bird's-foot shapes, and either solid green or variegated in white, cream, light green, yellow, or gold.

INTERESTING KINDS: There are many less-invasive ivies, including 'Ritterkreuz', and *H. colchica* 'Sulphur Heart', which if kept clipped to prevent mature development and seed production, can be maintained with less threat to nearby at-risk habitats.

NOT ALL IVIES ARE ALIKE. Note that some kinds, especially the fast-growing, large-leaf Algerian ivy (*H. canariensis*), and a generic "ivy-looking" ivy known as 'Pittsburgh' (*H. hibernica*), have become seriously invasive in some areas of California, where they creep or spread by seed into moist natural areas and can overwhelm native vegetation and disrupt wildlife.

 BOTTOM LINE: Be responsible if you choose to use hardy ivy in your garden—select a "good" kind, or substitute another evergreen groundcover such as Asiatic or star jasmine, or native manzanitas or creeping mahonia.

Ivy Geranium
Pelargonium peltatum
Sun or light shade

Though not effective as an erosion control, this hanging basket or container plant makes a decent groundcover or bank plant where drainage is good.

FLOWER: Rounded clusters of inch-wide single or double flowers in white, pink, rose, red, or lavender.

PLANT: Thick, glossy green, ivy-like leaves with pointed lobes are produced in abundance on foot-tall plants that sprawl or train up to 4 or 5 feet wide.

INTERESTING KINDS: The Summer Showers strain has flowers of mixed colors and can be grown from seed.

Kinnikinnick or Bearberry
Arctostaphylos uva-ursi
Sun or light shade

A popular kind of native manzanita groundcover that is slow to establish but eventually forms a wide, dense mat up to 15 feet across even on difficult slopes.

FLOWER: White or pinkish-white urn-shaped flowers followed by attractive red fruits favored by birds.

PLANT: Spreading flat mat of small, glossy leaves that turn red or purplish in cool winters, roots as it grows to form a colony. Pull weeds and use lots of mulch until established.

INTERESTING KINDS: 'Point Reyes' is very tolerant of heat and drought; 'Radiant' has large red berries; Little Sur manzanita (*A. edmundsii* 'Little Sur') makes a very dense groundcover with pointed leaves that have reddish margins and soft pink flowers.

Mondo Grass

Ophiopogon japonicus

Dense shade or filtered sun

Mondo or "little monkey grass" is a deep green grassy groundcover that spreads aggressively in the densest shade, even under oaks and evergreen shrubs. Use as a border or as a lawn substitute.

FLOWER: Inconspicuous spikes of pinkish white, bell-shaped flowers held close to the ground, usually hidden in the foliage but show up if mondo is mowed in the spring prior to flowering.

PLANT: Low-growing, arching, fine-textured (thin) leaves that are very dark green, produced in soft clumps that spread rapidly by runners.

INTERESTING KINDS: 'Nanus' is a very small, tight ball of foliage under 4 inches tall. *Ophiopogon planiscapus* 'Nigrescens' is slow spreading and nearly black. Foot-tall Aztec grass (*O. intermedius*) is a larger, more vigorous variegated form for difficult, dry settings.

Prostrate Rosemary

Rosmarinus officinalis

Sun

Very useful cascading forms of the classic Mediterranean shrub can be used as groundcovers on slopes, in raised beds, and even in parking lot dividers.

FLOWER: Edible blue or white small flowers held in clusters along the stem bloom winter and spring.

PLANT: Cascading evergreen with thin, almost conifer-like green leaves with gray undersides, very oily and aromatic, though most of the groundcover types are not particularly "tasty." Requires good drainage, and occasional pinching to keep it thick. Cuttings root readily.

INTERESTING KINDS: Very cold-hardy 'Irene', little more than a foot or so tall, spreads vigorously 2 or 3 feet per year; members of the Prostratus group are 2 feet tall but spread and cascade up to 8 feet; 'Collingwood Ingram' is too "piney" to use as seasoning but grows 2^1/$_2$ feet tall by 4 feet wide.

Rockrose
Cistus species
Sun

Fast growing and tolerant of extreme drought, these carefree grayish shrubs—very useful in fire hazard areas—are such low-growing, wide-spreaders that they make excellent groundcovers for low-water areas.

FLOWER: Showy 2- to $2^1/_2$-inch-wide, white, pink, purplish-pink flowers bloom mostly from spring to summer.

PLANT: Mounded, spreading shrubs with grayish, silvery, or wooly leaves, some with sticky perfumed resin. Can grow from seashore to mountain to desert—without irrigation. Thin out old stems to keep the plants vigorous.

INTERESTING KINDS: Sageleaf rockrose (*C. salviifolius*) grows up to 2 feet high and 6 feet wide, with crinkly, veined foliage and big white flowers; 'Brilliancy' or 'Sunset' has dark magenta flowers on plants that are 2 feet high and over 6 feet wide.

Trailing Coyote Brush
Baccharis pilularis
Sun

The most indestructible groundcover for flat or low-lying areas in hot sun, this California native thrives from the coast to high desert, on no water at all.

FLOWER: Separate male and female plants have small flowers, but female plants make messy cotton-like clusters of seed that blow around a lot; most named varieties are male clones.

PLANT: A fluffy but dense, light green mat from a few inches tall to 2 feet, but spreading rapidly to 6 or more feet wide.

INTERESTING KINDS: 'Twin Peaks' has darker green leaves; 'Pigeon Point' has larger, lighter green leaves and grows 2 feet high by over 8 feet wide. *Baccharis* 'Starn' is a female hybrid with tan seed capsules, tolerant of desert heat; it is the improved version of and replaces the old standard 'Centennial'.

81

Trailing Lantana
Lantana montevidensis
Sun

A super-dependable butterfly plant, this wide-spreading South American native has good winter cold tolerance but may not bloom in cool Fog Belt summers unless grown in a hot, dry exposure.

FLOWER: Tiny lavender-purple or white flowers open in showy, nearly flat clusters during warm weather.

PLANT: Sprawling vine-like stems; crinkly leaves have a pungent odor when crushed.

INTERESTING KINDS: 'Lavender Swirl' has a mixture of white and purple flowers; orange and pink 'Miss Huff' (*L. camara*) spreads up to 10 feet and is very cold hardy; wide-ranging 'New Gold' is a sterile hybrid that blooms nonstop during warm weather because it doesn't waste energy setting seed. Other spreaders include burnt orange 'Tangerine' and vivid orange-red 'Spreading Sunset'.

Wall Rockcress
Arabis alpina **ssp.** *caucasica*
Sun

Usually members of this plant group are used for rock gardens, edging, and "pattern" plantings. This long-popular species is hardy throughout California and spreads into a tight groundcover. It could be an interesting alternative groundcover for small spaces.

FLOWER: The groundcover is covered almost the entire spring in nearly solid white flowers.

PLANT: Gray-green and mat-forming, this species remains about 6 inches tall and spreads to nearly 2 feet wide. Like nearly all gray- or silvery-leaf plants, rockcress must have good drainage.

INTERESTING KINDS: 'Variegata' has gray leaves with creamy white margins; 'Flore Pleno' is double-flowered; 'Pink Charm' and 'Rosabella' have pink flowers. *Arabis procurrens* is another creeping species with white-flowering stems up to a foot tall.

Wintercreeper
Euonymus fortunei var. *radicans*
Sun or shade

In need of an ivy substitute? This commonly grown freeze-proof, desert-tolerant vine is a ground- or wall-hugging variation of the bigger shrub euonymus, very useful for erosion control and difficult areas (it is often used in cemeteries).

FLOWER: Not noticeable.

PLANT: A steady-spreading tight mass of thick evergreen leaves whose stems root where they touch the ground. Powdery mildew or scale insects can be troublesome, especially in foggy or over-watered areas; for control, simply stop watering as much and mow and rake the area to stimulate thick, healthy new growth.

INTERESTING KINDS: *Euonymus fortunei* 'Sunspot' has a bright yellow central blotch; purple-leaf wintercreeper 'Coloratus' gets 2 feet high and stays somewhat neat, with leaves turning dark purple in cool weather or winter.

Wooly Yarrow
Achillea tomentosa
Sun

Yarrows have been a mainstay of the herbal and perennial border for many years and are covered in the perennials chapter. But this one with gray-green, furry, fernlike foliage makes a good groundcover above strong spring bulbs or beneath a leggy crape myrtle or other light-shade trees.

FLOWER: Tight, flat cluster of small flowers on stems under a foot tall.

PLANT: Spreading mass to nearly 2 feet wide, with furry gray-green leaves. Easy to dig and divide for increasing or spreading. Requires very well-drained soil and occasional dividing when clumps get thick (easy to share with other gardeners or to increase your own groundcover).

INTERESTING KINDS: 'Primrose Beauty' has pale yellow flowers; 'King George' has creamy white blooms.

Other Good Groundcovers:

These are a few of the other great low-growing, spreading plants to fill up bare spaces. Some need a little extra care, are too unusual for mainstream gardeners, or are simply too untidy.

Aaron's Beard (*Hypericum calycinum*) is a durable creeping St. John's wort that spreads vigorously by underground stems into a tight, foot-tall mass of medium or light-green leaves and attractive bright yellow summer flowers. Competes well with tree roots in poor soils.

Blue Sedge (*Carex flacca, C. glauca*) is a slow-creeping, grass-like plant ranging from 6 inches to nearly 2 feet tall and wide, clumps spread slowly in sun or shade, tolerates some foot traffic and can be clipped like a lawn.

Catalina Perfume (*Ribes viburnifolium*) is a spreading native "sub-shrub" arching up to 3 feet tall, but spreads to over 10 feet wide. Light pink to purplish flowers in late winter or spring produce red berries, and roundish leaves have an apple or pine scent when bruised or even after a rain.

Catmint and **Catnip** (*Nepeta × faassennii* and *N. cataria*) may or may not make your cat ecstatic, but they can be divided or seeded (or self-seeded) into moderately dry areas as soft groundcovers with attractive flowers of white, pink, or lavender blue, loaded with butterflies and bees.

Chameleon Plant (*Houttuynia cordata*) is a powerful spreader, especially in moist areas—it is on the noxious weed list—with slick heart-shaped leaves that disappear completely in the winter, even in mild areas. The most common form has showy splashes of cream, pink, yellow, and red.

Cranesbill (*Erodium reichardii*) is a lot tougher than it looks, with dense foliage just a few inches tall and small, dark green roundish leaves with scalloped edges and many flowers of white, rose pink, or yellow flowers from early spring into fall. Great for small areas or rock gardens.

Goldmoss Sedum (*Sedum acre*) is a delicate-looking succulent with small, narrow, pale green evergreen leaves and showy sprays of yellow spring flowers. Tough enough to grow in a cemetery urn. Use between stepping stones or tucked into dry rock walls. It's a nice weed.

Indian Strawberry (*Duchesnea indica*) is a trailing evergreen with stems that root as they grow along the ground. Flowers are yellow, followed by tasteless (but not poisonous) red fruit that is held above the foliage. Use under shrubs and trees that are not well watered.

Kenilworth Ivy (*Cymbalaria muralis*) is a weedy ivy-like trailing vine for the shade, with toothed leaves and mostly-spring lilac blue flowers at leaf joints. Grows anywhere.

Korean Grass (*Zoysia tenuifolia*) is an outstanding meadow-like lawn substitute in areas that are difficult to mow or irrigate. Turns a uniform tan in cool weather, greens up late in the spring.

Best for Beginners:

- *Asiatic Jasmine*
- *Creeping Junipers*
- *Ivy Geranium*
- *Mondo Grass*
- *Wintercreeper Euonymus*

Kinda Tricky:

- *Ajuga*
- *Cotoneaster* (requires weeding while young)
- *Dwarf Ruellia* (slow to spread)
- *Ivy* (choose non-invasive kinds)
- *Ivy Geranium*
- *Trailing Lantana*

Mazus (*Mazus reptans*) is a mere 2 inches tall but spreads over a foot with stems that root as they creep across the ground. Tolerates foot traffic when planted between stepping stones. Flowers are purple-blue with yellow and white markings, and appear in pairs from spring to summer.

Redwood Sorrel (*Oxalis oregana*) is a steady-spreading California woodland (shade-loving) native with velvety green three-leaflet foliage and white or pink, lavender-streaked spring flowers. Tolerates moisture and either dies down in winter or can be sheared to rejuvenate tired patches.

Seashore Paspalum (*Paspalum vaginatum* 'Adalayd') is an informal warm-season turf, very tolerant of foot traffic as well as high temperatures, and saline in the water and soil. Use in informal seashore landscapes, dog runs, and pockets of light shade.

Sweet Alyssum

Showy Evening Primrose (*Oenothera speciosa*) is a dependable native with showy pink or white flowers, very sturdy in zero-maintenance areas, but much-hated by gardeners who ever try to control its rampant growth. Makes a loose groundcover.

Snow-in-Summer (*Cerastium tomentosum*) is a low-growing, dense mat of silvery gray, 6 to 8 inches high and spreading 3 feet a year. Masses of small white flowers in summer provide its common name. Plant is not long-lived but divides and replants easily.

Sweet Alyssum (*Lobularia maritima*) is a showy but invasive annual that can fill areas of very poor soil and no water—even in parking lot dividers.

Trailing African Daisy (*Osteospermum fruticosum*) is not called "freeway daisy" for nothing—the rapidly-spreading, foot-tall plant has showy flowers of lilac, purple, white-and-blue, dark pink, yellow, and others, depending on cultivar, nearly all year long.

Variegated Dwarf Bamboo (*Pleioblastus chino* var. *argenteostriatus*) is a steady-spreading variegated bamboo that stays under 3 feet tall, very good for shaded areas where sturdy borders prevent its spread.

Wooly Gazania (*Dymondia margaretae*) is a tight, mat-forming gray-green plant with cottony white undersides to the leaves, less than 3 or 4 inches tall with yellow daisy-like summer flowers that are nearly hidden in the foliage.

Give Them an Inch ... and they'll steal your entire landscape!

Some terrific groundcovers can be so prolific they take more than their fair share of the land and can be the hardest plants to keep in bounds (with or without weed killers), including: Chameleon Plant, Goldmoss Sedum, Kenilworth Ivy, Indian Strawberry, Sweet Alyssum, Variegated Dwarf Bamboo, Showy Evening Primrose, Asiatic Jasmine, Ajuga, English Ivy, Algerian Ivy, Mondo grass, Dwarf Vinca. Think two or three times before choosing them, or don't complain about the results!

Gardeners' Bill of Rights

Hard-core gardeners are as misunderstood as those people who wear costumes and paint and goofy hats to professional football games. Difference is, gardeners can't wash off the greasepaint come Monday morning.

Still, we are a proud tribe of unique individuals and we expect to be treated with the respect that comes from hard work on our private property. Here is my starting point, a suggested bill of basic rights for freeing us from the oppression of neighbors.

GARDENERS SHALL HAVE:

- The right to plant stuff in the front yard, away from the foundation of the house.
- The right to as many wind chimes as we can afford. Bird feeders, too. And a porch swing. (A couch on the front porch is not covered under this bill of rights.)
- The right to have no grass at all, except maybe a little patch so you can lie on your back and watch the sky.
- The right to not hear lawn mowers before 10:00 in the morning.
- The right to more potted plants than we can water, and to plant too many tomatoes every year.
- The right to a leaf pile, if not an outright compost system.
- The right to mispronounce plant names (and to use the H in herbs).
- The right to cultivate plants others consider "weeds."
- The right to plant any color of flower next to any other color flower, even if they clash.
- The right to prune or not to prune leggy plants—with no questions asked.
- The right to garden at any hour, day or night.
- The right to display inexpensive or home-made garden accessories, including but not limited to plastic birds, naked statuary, and reflective orbs. Amendment: Gnomes are not covered in this bill, because they have their own rights.
- The right to wear big floppy hats and loose clothing—no matter how ridiculous we look.
- The right to show our behinds to neighbors as we bend over digging and planting (except where applicable local indecency laws may be in effect.

Herbs
OR 'ERBS?

Herbs put the zing in teas and the zest in sauces; they are the essence in soups and the fragrance of potpourri. And some provide soothing or stimulating medicinal benefits. Still, there is nothing magic about herb plants; they are simply "value added"—they perform double duty as decent garden plants, plus a little extra for their herbal uses.

You don't need to have a herb garden to grow and enjoy herb plants. If you don't actually use them as herbs, they become "ordinary" perennials, annuals, or shrubs that blend into the overall garden scheme. Treat them as specimen plants (bay trees and rosemary shrubs, highlighted in other chapters, come to mind), use them as accents or border plants or groundcovers, or grow them in pots.

To get the very most out of herbs, there are a couple of simple concepts to keep in mind:

- What gives most herb plants their special benefits are oils, which are more concentrated in plants that are kept "lean and mean"—too much water or fertilizer causes leggy growth and lessens the potency of the oils.

- And regular harvesting keeps them on their toes, constantly putting out new growth that increases both their garden interest and their herbal usefulness.

Everything else about growing herb plants—for their unique beauty or for herbal benefits—boils down to the basics of just good gardening.

Herbs in a Children's Garden Outside Fillmore, California

Angelica

Angelica archangelica

Sun

Looking like a coarse Queen Anne's lace, various parts of this spring-blooming biennial or short-lived perennial have been used for centuries as flavoring (for wine, gin, and vermouth), herbal tea, salads, cakes and desserts, and perfumes and soaps.

FLOWER: Greenish-yellow flowers in slightly rounded clusters tower above everything else in the garden.

PLANT: Upright, 5 or 6 feet tall and wide, tropical-looking plant with fat stems. Bright green leaves are made up of three large, finely toothed leaflets. Needs to be planted in a moist area or ditch bank, especially in hot-sun areas of the state.

Anise

Pimpinella anisum

Sun

Seeds of this tender annual are used in baking and confections, and leaves are eaten as salad greens. Plants grow quickly from seed sown the spring. Seeds or plants can also be planted in late summer in hot-summer areas.

FLOWER: Airy clusters of tiny white flowers at tips of stems.

PLANT: Annual with heart-shaped leaves in clumps, ferny leaves on flowering stems to 2 feet tall or taller. The plant doesn't look like much by itself, so grow it in a big group or with other, sturdier plants.

Basil
Ocimum basilicum
Sun

This popular summer herb loves summer heat (which is hard to find sometimes in the Fog Belt), and hates cool springs and falls. And it is a water hog. Still, its many colorful forms are all useful in a wide variety of cooked dishes, sauces, and anything with tomatoes in it—even sprinkled on raw slices.

FLOWER: Sometimes-showy clusters of white or purple spikes held above the foliage all season; pinch them off for more foliage, or leave them on for bees to enjoy.

PLANT: Upright annual that can be tight or open, globe-shaped or sprawling, with leaves of green, deep burgundy, purple, or variegated. In cool areas grow against a south-facing wall so the basil can enjoy the collected heat.

Borage
Borago officinalis
Sun or part shade

Having trouble growing cucumbers? The large leaves of this European herb are a fair substitute—for flavor, if not "mouth feel." As a bonus, its incredibly blue flowers are also edible.

FLOWER: Branched stems rising above the foliage have clusters of bright blue flowers in the summer and early fall, which attract tons of bees. Cut flowers as a garnish, or at least snip the faded clusters before they go to seed, or you may have more borage plants than you want. Save a few seed to sow the next spring.

PLANT: Rounded clump of large bristly gray-green leaves up to 6 inches long. Good drought tolerance but grows much better with an occasional soaking. Mulch beds to conserve moisture and to prevent extra seedlings.

Chives

Allium schoenoprasum

Sun

This dependable perennial provides year-round fresh leaves with a distinct onion flavor; the plant can survive every weather extreme California can dump on it.

FLOWER: Small round lavender clusters of edible flowers on thin stems in spring.

PLANT: Thick clump of hollow grass-like leaves to a foot or more grow from small bulbs, very easy to divide any time.

Cilantro or Coriander

Coriandrum sativum

Sun or light shade

When leaves are used in salads and cooked dishes they are called cilantro; when seeds are collected and use for seasoning cooked dishes, they are called coriander.

FLOWER: Flat clusters of white or pinkish flowers are produced in the summer, and then the plant dies.

PLANT: Airy, ferny plant that does not last into hot weather, but self-sows easily. You can plant seed in the spring, or again in late summer in hot-summer areas. Keep cool and moist.

Is It Herb or Erb?

Most people use the "H" when they say "herbs" for one reason only: because that's how they have always 'eard it pronounced. The English use the H, the French drop it. Truth is, according to the Herb Society of America, it can go E-ther or I-ther way. My way of looking at it—the only time you are "wrong" is when you correct someone else. Me, I say herb with an H for one reason: It's got an H in it!

Dill
Anethum graveolens
Sun

Seeds are used in vinegars and pickles; young seedlings and fresh leaves are used in salads, sauces, and cooked dishes.

FLOWER: Pale yellow flowers are held in umbrella-like clusters up to 6 inches across in the summer (or in the winter in the desert).

PLANT: Feathery, fragrant leaves on airy plants to 4 feet tall. Sow seeds in late winter or early spring or in the fall in hot desert areas. Plant self-sows for years and can actually become kind of weedy.

Florence Fennel or Finocchio
Foeniculum vulgare var. *azoricum*
Sun

This is NOT the invasive weedy fennel, but its tossed-and-lost seeds may germinate and revert to the weedy type. This annual is grown for its thick leaf stalks that are eaten raw or cooked. Its seeds are used for baking.

FLOWER: Same as the common fennel, flat clusters of yellow flowers in the summer.

PLANT: Fern-like leaves whose stalks are thick and bulb-like at their base. You can plant seed in the spring or again in late summer in hot-summer areas.

Garlic Chives

Allium tuberosum

Sun

Closely related to onions and chives, but with moderate garlic flavor and smell, very tough in either containers or as a flower border edging. May seed about in the garden.

FLOWER: Loose cluster of sweetly scented white flowers in summer atop thin stems, good for flower arrangements, fresh or dry.

PLANT: Spreading mass of narrow, flattened grass-like leaves to a foot or so high. Can survive in containers without water for months.

Lemon Balm

Melissa officinalis

Sun or light shade

Leaves of this southern Europe native are lemon-scented and used fresh in drinks, salads, fruit cups, and fish dishes, or dried for potpourri or sachets.

FLOWER: Airy heads of not-showy flowers in the summer. Seeds are prolific enough for plants to become a pest.

PLANT: Upright to nearly 3 feet tall, many-branched with light-green, heavily-veined (almost ruffled) pointed ovals to 3 or 4 inches long, in pairs. Golden or variegated forms are available.

Marjoram
Origanum marjorana
Sun

Leaves of this very tender perennial, which is almost universally grown as an annual, are used fresh or dried to season scrambled eggs, casseroles, salads, meat dishes, and tomato dishes.

FLOWER: Knot-like clusters of tiny white flowers should be cut off to keep plants sprouting fresh new leaf growth.

PLANT: Sow seeds in spring or in the fall where summers get hot early, or grow potted plants indoors over the winter. Oval grayish leaves give away this plant's Mediterranean origins. 'White Anniversary' has a creamy white border around each leaf.

Mexican Mint Marigold
Tagetes lucida
Sun or part sun

This Mexican native—a true perennial marigold—makes a fine tarragon substitute, giving it its other common name of Mexican tarragon. It is often planted in Hispanic or Mexican cemeteries for its showy orange-yellow flowers at the beginning of November, right on time for Day of the Dead festivities.

FLOWER: Buttery yellow flowers less than a half-inch long are produced in clusters in the fall.

PLANT: Multiple-stem clump dense with narrow, unbranched stems 2 to 3 feet tall, with many narrow leaves that smell strongly of licorice when crushed.

Mint

Mentha species

Sun

As aggressive a genus as anyone could want, old stands of mint can be found around abandoned homesteads, having survived with no care for many years. Leaves are used for making teas, seasoning, refreshing drinks, potpourri, and making medicine go down a little better.

FLOWER: Sometimes-showy pale blue to purplish spikes at ends of stems, good for bees.

PLANT: Perennial with aggressive underground stems that sprout at every joint into upward-growing leafy stems. Leaves are oval or pointed, intensely fragrant with essential oils. There are many "flavors" including spearmint, apple, orange, peppermint, and chocolate.

Oregano

Origanum vulgare

Sun or light shade

Grown for its leaves, use fresh or dried in many Italian and Mexican dishes. Many different varieties abound. Pass up the nearly unscented, generic seed-grown wild oregano and choose either the pungent Greek oregano (*O. vulgare* ssp. *hirtum*), or milder but more colorful forms that are grown from cuttings. Scratch and sniff before purchasing.

FLOWER: Small but somewhat showy white or purplish-pink flowers in summer.

PLANT: Perennial spreading mass of upright stems covered with oval leaves that are very pungent. Greek oregano has broader, slightly furry, gray-green leaves.

Parsley
Petroselinum crispum
Sun

Used as a garnish with a twist—even a small piece of fresh leaf can be chewed to instantly and completely erase "garlic mouth" after a spicy meal.

FLOWER: Tall stems topped with airy umbrella-like clusters of yellow. Peel and cook the lower flower stems like you would asparagus.

PLANT: Mound of bright green leaves with either smooth or ruffled edges. The cold-tolerant plants grow better with a little winter chill, so plant in fall even in areas that freeze in the winter, or set out transplants in late winter. For the most intense parsley flavor, stick with Italian flat-leaf or plain-leaf types.

Sage
Salvia officinalis
Sun or light shade

Leaves are used in many different dishes.

FLOWER: Loose spikes of lavender, blue, violet, pink, or white in the late spring.

PLANT: Low-growing, spreading perennial with very pungent oblong, wrinkled leaves. Several quality kinds are widely available, with foliage that includes solid gray-green, reddish-purple, golden-edged, and tricolor with green, cream, and purplish pink. All require good soil drainage.

Summer Savory
Satureja species
Sun or light shade

Thyme-like leaves are used for flavoring soups, beans, and other cooked vegetables, meats, fish, and egg dishes.

FLOWER: Tiny pinkish-white flowers in summer, not showy.

PLANT: Summer annual or short lived perennial; plant in the spring. Narrow aromatic leaves on an upright plant to under 2 feet tall.

NOTE: Winter savory (*S. montana*) is a shrubby perennial useful in rock gardens or as a small hedge, but has a stronger flavor than summer savory. Also, dried leaves of the related *yerba buena* (*S. douglasii*), a California native perennial groundcover, have long been used as a stimulating tea.

Thyme
Thymus vulgaris
Sun or light shade

There are many different kinds of thyme, including several used for flavoring soups, vegetables, poultry, fish, stuffing, and more. Choose carefully.

FLOWER: Delicate white, lilac, or purple flowers in spring and summer.

PLANT: Creeping or fast-spreading tight carpet of small aromatic leaves. Requires good drainage.

 Best for Beginners:

- Chives
- Garlic Chives
- Mexican Mint Marigold
- Mint
- Oregano
- Rosemary

Kinda Tricky:

- Anise
- Fennel
- Parsley
- Sage
- Thyme

Slow Gardening

Has your waistline been supersized while your garden interest has withered? In just a couple or three generations we've gone from eating mostly home-cooked food and growing stuff mostly under our own power, to routine fast-food and "mow-and-blow" landscapes. Sure, we've shed a lot of the menial work, but at what cost to the connections with the Earth and family and friends that our ancestors took for granted?

THE MAIN THING IS TO KEEP THE MAIN THING THE MAIN THING

Slow gardening to the rescue! Similar to Slow Food™ (www.slowfoodusa.org), an international movement of convivial connoisseurs who savor producing and preparing in-season dishes, a "slow gardening" approach can help us better enjoy our gardens year in and year out, and possibly connect us with our neighbors.

How to be a Slow Gardener? Think "long haul" and take your time. Life has lots of pressures—why include them in the garden? Anything that helps us garden without causing extra-sweaty exertion is always welcome—especially if it is simple enough for the gardener to be the only moving part! Simple tools and simple motions, for simple pleasures.

Start a compost or leaf pile and recycle kitchen scraps, and install a rain barrel. Keep a bird feeder well-stocked. Make a working garden swing (hint: the longer the chain, the slower and more relaxing the ride).

Grow plants that like your climate, and that provide something for local wildlife. Include attractive vegetables, fruits, and herbs that double as ornamentals; plan ahead so you can harvest them and enjoy their flowers as long as possible, with as little effort as practical. Look around in every season, then plant what has traditionally done well with ease. Plant heirlooms that multiply readily so you can share with others.

Gardeners have always been a sharing tribe; it rarely takes long for us to start chatting about weather, which can quickly lead to a smile about something to do with gardening. Before you know it, your garden could have plants shared by seed, rooted cuttings, or divisions, from all over the neighborhood.

Get outside, but take it slow and easy. Lightening up doesn't necessarily mean lowering your standards!

Patio Plants
WITH PANACHE

This chapter deals with the many great plants that are "typically" grown in containers everywhere, even those that are able to survive outdoors in the ground in some areas.

Most of us learned at an early age how to grow plants in pots, from the first time a school teacher showed us how to put a bean seed in a milk carton. We learned to give it a little sunshine, some water when it got dry, and a little "plant food" to help it grow. Then it usually died, which set us up for expecting failure with poinsettias and African violets given to us as gifts. And when we or a family member came home from the hospital with one of those mixed pots of baby tropical plants—usually a heart-leaf philodendron, a small palm, a mother-in-law's tongue, and a prayer plant—the prayer plant quickly gave up the ghost.

Without realizing it, we began learning about tough plants, because that mother-in-law's tongue (*Sansevieria*) survived, and the heart-leaf philodendron vine began spreading all around the window. Those simple plants taught us that some potted creatures actually thrive in the low-light, low-humidity, and cool-temperature spaceship environments we call home. And quite a few are perfectly happy outdoors in our gardens, usually in the shade where they find their natural jungle-like environment.

Bromeliads

California Is Not All Subtropical

In spite of the palms, Norfolk Island pines, and bromeliads we see in Southern California, where tropical plantings around service stations and shopping malls are the norm, most of California is a tricky place for growing tropical plants. Even along parts of the coast, and especially just a few miles inland, many great landscape plants get nipped in the winter.

Still, many popular plants from the tropics are grown outdoors in pots than can be brought indoors if need be for a night or two. This chapter highlights some of the toughest, easiest to grow, longest-lived tropical plants that are hardy in most of the state, or grown as potted plants everywhere.

Lots of other types of plants are also ideal for containers. Many desert plants need perfect soil drainage or they can rot. Potting soils can be created that are right for each kind, and watering in a pot is more exact than in the yard where sprinklers

Dwarf Schefflera and Shell Ginger

drench everything within the Colorado River's reach. Some plants are too weedy for the yard, and quite simply cannot be safely grown "in-ground" — mint, some ivies, running-type bamboo, chameleon plant, and goldmoss sedum come to mind. How better to keep an eye on them than when they are surrounded with patio paving? Lastly, there are also many compact trees and shrubs, from 'Little Gem' magnolia to dwarf fruit trees and shrub roses, that are best viewed up close. Containers bring them into focus and make caring for them a little easier than when they're stuck out in the "back forty."

Environmental and Cultural Needs

Location, location, location! Most container plants grow in widely varying conditions, but do best if provided three basic conditions: bright indirect light, humidity, and protection from freezing. Once those parameters are met, how you take care of your plants can determine the difference between their thriving and merely surviving. Water, fertilizer, and occasional repotting are about all they need.

Too wet is worse than too dry—water "as needed." Variations in environmental conditions, plant type, pot size, potting soil type, and the amount of fertilizer used will cause plants to grow at different rates and need water in varying amounts.

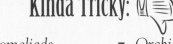

Best for Beginners:

- *Airplane Plant*
- *Asparagus Fern*
- *Bird of Paradise*
- *Chinese Evergreen*
- *Devil's Backbone*
- *Dwarf Schefflera*
- *Ponytail Palm*

Kinda Tricky:

- *Bromeliads (some types)*
- *Citrus*
- *Elephant Ears*
- *Orchids (some types)*
- *Staghorn Fern*

Fertilize plants a very little at a time—I use a good timed-release fertilizer (the long-lasting fertilizer beads) once in the spring, then occasionally hit the plants with a light shot of liquid plant food containing "trace minerals" (iron, zinc, calcium, etc., listed on the side of the container). NOTE: Use plant foods at one-half the recommended strength—the directions on the containers indicate the absolute highest application amounts, which are simply not necessary for good plant growth.

Repotting should be done when plants have been in the same worn-out potting soil for years or when the plant has gotten too big for its pot. My personal potting soil recipe, which I came up with while researching various mixes in college, holds up a long time, keeps plants upright in the pots, stays moist without staying wet, and holds nutrients so they don't wash out too quickly. It is easy to make and inexpensive. I mix it on the driveway and store it in a plastic garbage can.

INGREDIENTS: One part cheap potting soil and one part finely ground bark mulch. That's it. The bark allows good water and air penetration; the potting soil holds moisture and nutrients. Sometimes I put a few rocks in the bottom of pots to help keep top-heavy plants from tipping over.

Angel's Trumpet
Brugmansia species

Several species and named cultivars of this tropical monster, all hardy in the ground in warm-winter areas, but leave a large visual hole when they are dormant in most places. Container-grown plants have extra height and can be moved around when looking ratty from wind or weather, or wintered over in a garage with little water or sunlight.

Airplane Plant or Spider Plant
Chlorophytum comosum

One of the most popular hanging basket plants, airplant plants are also used as a bedding groundcover. It makes a sprawling clump of long, narrow, arching, grass-like leaves, either solid green or variegated, and sends out 2- or 3-foot flowering stems covered with $1/2$-inch white flowers and miniature plantlets, each of which can be cut off and quickly rooted into a new plant.

103

Asparagus Fern

Asparagus densiflorus
Sprengeri Group

One of the easiest, most drought-tolerant potted plants around, this false fern is a member of the lily family, closely related to edible asparagus. Long cascading "fronds" make it an ideal companion for other tropical plants, in-ground or spilling from containers. Tiny, needle-like leaflets give the arching stems a light-green billowy effect. Hard white tubers which help the plant get through long periods of drought can be cut off when repotting. Popular relative is 'Myersii' asparagus fern, which produces many dense, nearly cylindrical upright spikes of darker green leaves.

Baby Rubber Plant

Peperomia obtusifolia

Bushy, multi-stem plant to a foot or more tall and wide with succulent stems and smooth, glossy, deep green leaves up to 4 inches long with a notch near the end. Flowers are small but on interesting cord-like spikes. Very sensitive to frost damage; often grown simply as a durable "house" plant. 'Variegata' has wide, irregular creamy white leaf margins. Others include watermelon peperomia (*P. sandersii*) and emerald ripple peperomia (*P. caperata*). Prefers shade to part shade.

Bird of Paradise
Strelitzia reginae

Though ground-hardy only in mild-winter areas—it can take frost but not a deep or prolonged freeze—this striking specimen with bizarre flowers of orange, blue, and white is very easy to grow in a moderate-size pot (plants bloom best when crowded or root-bound). It can take full sun or part shade, and flowers last for many weeks, opening one orange "crest" at a time.

Brazilian Plume
Justicia carnea

This soft-wooded tropical shrub has long leaves with prominent veins that create a lush backdrop for the thick spikes 6 inches or more tall studded with 2-inch tubular flowers of crimson or pink in the summer and fall. 'Huntington Form' has deep pink flowers and leaves that are bronzy colored underneath.

Bromeliads
Many genera

The large "pineapple" family includes mostly stemless plants with clustered leaves, many of which are handsomely marked. Flower clusters often have colorful, long-lasting bracts. Most are epiphytes (grow in trees) while others are semi-terrestrial (grow in the ground or well-drained potting soil). Those that hold water in their central cups should not be kept wet indoors or the water can stagnate and cause rot. Some of the more commonly grown bromeliads are briefly described here but there are many, many others.

Best Bets for Beginners:

Tillandsias are mostly epiphytes, some with very showy flowers. Common natives are Spanish moss (*T. usneoides*) and ball moss (*T. recurvata*). These are grown mostly by exotic plant collectors who like to hang them from trees, not plant them in containers.

Aechmea bromeliads grow in the shape of urns or rosettes that can hold water and grow best in fast-draining potting soil. No need to keep the central vase filled with water or rot may occur.

Ananas comosus is the familiar pineapple, a terrestrial bromeliad that is easy to grow as a plant but may take two or more years to produce a flowering (fruiting) stem. Grow plants from tops cut off mature fruits, rooted in shallow water. Variegated form is very showy.

Billbergias are usually tall, slender urn-shaped epiphytes with variegated, banded, mottled, colorful foliage and cutting-quality flowers. Easy to divide. Can even be used as groundcovers.

Cryptanthus bromeliads are commonly called "earth stars" for their flattened rosettes of narrow leaves usually banded or striped. They grow best in very porous potting soils.

Neoregelias are striking epiphytes that grow as rosettes of stiff leaves with white or blue flowers that extend just above the water in the center of the cupped leaves. The central portion often turns rosy red. Spiny-edge leaves can have red spots or leaf tips.

Chinese Evergreen
Aglaonema species

Chinese evergreen thrives in offices and airports where all other plants have slowly wasted away; they are similarly well adapted to the home's very low light and low humidity. Small, canna-like plants have several sturdy upright stems of narrow, sword-like leaves up to a foot or more long that are glossy and often variegated. Tricolor 'Silverado' can brighten the darkest corner. One of the most durable "house" plants.

Chinese Hibiscus
Hibiscus rosa-sinensis

Hate to put such a wonderful plant in a pot, especially when it grows so well on the street. But because not everyone can grow a 15-foot hedge with this frost-sensitive plant, it remains one of the standard tropical plants for large containers. Deep green or variegated, smooth or ruffled leaves, single flowers or double, the plant is available in an astounding array of colors and combinations. Pinching stem tips helps keep plants contained. 'White Wings' may be the most dependable old standard for cool-weather areas.

Clivia
Clivia miniata

This is an almost irresistible plant collector's favorite for its ease of propagation as well as its showy flowers and red-berried seed clusters. Though it grows best where summer nights are cool, it will freeze quite easily and must be brought in during the winter. Flowers best if fed regularly and kept root-bound. Gardeners often hide the non-blooming potted plants under a bench.

Copperleaf
Acalypha wilkesiana

This woody perennial, grown as a small or medium-size shrub in warm-winter areas, is more dependably colorful over a longer period of time than many flowers. Its large green leaves are splotched and mottled, according to variety, with combinations of bronze, purple, crimson, orange, and red. The leaves are sturdy enough that if the plant wilts from a lack of water, a little spritz will pick it right back up. Very heat and wind tolerant.

Creeping Jenny
Lysimachia nummularia

This fast-spreading groundcover plant has many spreading stems of nearly overlapping pairs of round leaves up to an inch across. Most are light green, but 'Aurea' has chartreuse leaves that contrast well with darker plants. It creeps in and around everything, and may be best kept from taking over if planted in a container, as a trailing or cascading companion to other plants.

Dracaena
Dracaena species

The "corn" plant (*D. fragrans*) is often sold as a tiered, multiple-stemmed specimen, with each stem up to 3 inches in diameter and topped with a large whorl of long, downward-curving leaves, each up to 3 feet long and 4 inches wide. 'Massangeana' has a broad yellow stripe down the center of each leaf and is a common "house" plant. Others are smaller with thinner leaves, usually forming topknots on tall narrow stems. Ribbon dracaena (*D. sanderiana*) is small and white- or yellow-variegated. The popular "Chinese good luck bamboo" is simply a ribbon dracaena leaned at different angles during growth to produce twisted or spiral stems.

Dragonwing Begonia
Begonia 'Dragon Wing'

This fairly new hybrid begonia, a cross between the old-fashioned, leggy angelwing begonia and the durable compact wax begonia, has vigorous, glossy green leaves on sturdy but succulent stems up to 2 feet tall, very tolerant of a wide range of growing conditions. It is continuously covered with big loose clusters of red or pink flowers. 'Baby Wing Pink' is more compact with smaller leaves, and makes a companion to nearly anything in a pot.

Dumb Cane
Dieffenbachia species

Swallowing even a small amount of this plant's sap can paralyze the voice box, leaving a person unable to talk for hours—which is the source of the common name. Bold, wide, pointed leaves can be striking with variegations, stripes, edging, and spots of white, yellow, chartreuse, or cream. Tall plants can be cut back severely to force strong new growth near the base; the cut-off portions are easily rooted. Grown indoors only in most parts of California.

Dwarf Schefflera
Schefflera arboricola

This tidy little shrub, not as overwhelming as the taller umbrella schefflera, has leathery, deep green, hand-sized, many-fingered leaves, sometimes variegated. The plant tends to get branchy and quite leggy in low light, but pruning thickens it right back up. 'Gold Capella' has deep green, shiny oval leaves with contrasting intensely yellow variegation. The heat-tolerant plants can be used as large bedding plants or potted specimens.

Elephant's Ear or Taro
Alocasia, Colocasia, Xanthosoma

These nearly-gaudy Victorian favorites, used as centerpieces in large container "arrangements" (like canna, only bolder), typify the tropics with striking foliage, usually green but often variegated, chartreuse, or nearly black. Many fantastic selections, all great for large containers or moist areas in the garden. Snip off wind-tattered leaves as needed.

Hawaiian Ti
Cordyline fruticosa

This gaudy potted plant, hardy outdoors in mild areas, does best in warm, humid locations. Sometimes used as a showy understory planting where hot colors are needed or acceptable, its long, pointed leaves are fairly wide in the center and usually striped with red, yellow, or near-magenta. Sections of the thin dracaena-like stems are very easy to root. The larger, hardier "giant dracaena" (*C. australis*) has several very colorful cultivars.

Mother-in-Law's Tongue or Snake Plant
Sansevieria trifasciata

Talk about tough—this succulent from Africa can grow in an ashtray on top of the TV! And go months without water. I have collected many different kinds of *Sansevieria* (sans-see-VAIR-ee-uh); some are still alive after minimal care for over thirty years in the same pots. Rhizome-like runner stems can be divided or allowed to spread into a groundcover that can actually be hard to get rid of. Very tough plants. Can grow in very bright light or very low light.

Orchids
Many genera and hybrids

With over 17,000 species of orchids, perhaps the largest family in the plant kingdom, there naturally has to be at least one for every California gardener to grow. Nearly all of the "epiphytes" (air plants) are grown in pots or small hanging baskets filled with bark, or wired onto on "rafts" of wood. A few "terrestrial" kinds are grown in very well-drained potting soil mixed with bark.

Getting started with orchids is easy—just buy a few and keep them humid, moist (not wet), and lightly fed with liquid plant food. Commercial orchid soils and fertilizers take away a lot of guesswork.

Best Bets for Beginners:

Laelia anceps is hardy enough to grow outdoors even up to the San Francisco area, with long leaves and 4-inch pink or other color "corsage" type flowers. Related to cattleyas.

Cattleya orchids are among the most popular for their ease of culture and large "corsage" flowers. Dark growing conditions turn them dark green but make them soft.

Dendrobium orchids need a little direct sunshine. Some types have a nearly-dormant winter period during which they lose their leaves and need very little water.

Phalaenopsis, the "moth" orchid, has thick, leathery leaves and long sprays of large flowers up to 6 inches wide. They are terrestrial and need a well-drained potting soil.

Cymbidium and *Zygopetalum* are terrestrial orchids (grow in containers) with long, narrow, grasslike leaves and long-lasting flowers on arching spikes. They can tolerate very cool weather.

Oncidium orchids include a wide range of terrestrial orchids that grow in pots or in tree hollows.

Other good outdoor container orchids: *Bletilla*, *Calanthe*, *Encyclia*, *Epidendrum*, *Phaius*, and *Pleione*.

Philodendron
Philodendron species

Grown for their glossy leaves, this diverse but durable genus of tropical vines and subshrubs includes some of the most common houseplants in the country, and most are winter-hardy outdoors along California's mild-winter coast. Very few gardeners ever see a philodendron flower, which is a creamy white, calla-like spathe hidden within the foliage canopy. The foliage is glossy, slick (almost rubbery), and durable even in low humidity. Most grow best in bright but indirect light. Split-leaf philodendron (*P. bipinnatifidum*) has huge, elephant-ear leaves, deeply divided almost to the midrib, produced from a stocky, trunk-like vine with incredibly strong aerial roots used for support. It and a near relative, *Monstera deliciosa* (which often has holes in the leaves like Swiss cheese) can grow 6 to 8 feet tall in a pot, with leaves up to 3 feet long; 'Xanadu' is a super-tough "dwarf" form used in mass plantings, groundcovers, or as a potted specimen for low-light, low-humidity, breezy spots.

Plumeria
Plumeria rubra

Exotic "frangipani" trees may be hardy outdoors in many areas but they can suffer from too much care. The worst thing, other than cold weather, is too much water; keeping them in a container makes them easier to maintain. Many outstanding varieties are commonly available. Remember: Not too much care.

Ponytail Palm
Nolina recurvata

I have had one of these Mexican yucca relatives in the same pot for nearly twenty-five years, with at most a monthly soaking. It can withstand short dips into the teens. It is best kept in a pot or planted in very well drained sandy soil so excess rainfall won't cause soft spots to develop on its large bulbous base. The topknot of foliage can be a fountain of narrow leaves that hang down 3 feet or more.

Rubber T
Ficus e

Sturdy and bold, this tropical giant towers above homes in Southern California, but is quite often still grown as a potted plant for bold texture indoors or outside where its roots can be a problem in the ground. Glossy, flattened, football-shaped leaves can be green, burgundy, or have red stems and midribs; a variegated form is especially beautiful for lower light areas where a bold, durable splash is needed. Pruning forces new stems to come out right at the cut, which thickens the plants into shrubs.

Shell Ginger
Alpinia zerumbet

This compact ginger is not as winter-hardy in cold-winter areas as its *Hedychium* cousins, but makes a dramatic accent when splayed out in a pot. Hanging clusters of white, shell-like flowers are extra attractive in the spring and early summer.

Silver Falls Dichondra
Dichondra argentea 'Silver Falls'

Not your usual creeping green dichondra that you either love as a groundcover, or hate as a weed in your lawn, this dramatic cascading vine is a welcome plant in any container garden. Its long, draping, branching stems are covered with round, coin-size leaves that are a shimmering silver-gray. It tolerates heat and drought, making it perfect for pots with other heat-loving plants that need good drainage.

Sour-Acid Mandarin
× *Citrofortunella microcarpa*

Not everyone has room—or the best climate—for growing citrus at home, but this compact plant (as well as kumquats) has smaller, more abundant fruit and can be grown on a sunny porch or patio, or even indoors near a window. Also called calamondin orange.

Staghorn Fern
Platycerium bifurcatum

This is the monster of the low-light garden, hanging from a tree like an alien creature, or leering from a wall with menacing antler-like fronds. The "body" of this air fern is made of papery "sterile" fronds that enclose a little potting soil and other organic debris, which helps hold moisture between soakings. An old staghorn is a prized possession.

Wandering Jew
Tradescantia species

There are several commonly grown trailing plants in this group, all of which have rapidly-growing, juicy stems that snap off easily (also easy to root), covered with generally pointy-oval leaves. The plants come in plain green or variegated with white stripes, yellow stripes, or leaves banded in white and pale lavender. *Tradescantia fluminensis* 'Aurea' has bright yellow-green foliage. The three-petalled white flowers are not very showy. Prefers shade to part shade.

Wax Plant
Hoya carnosa

This trailing vine, which can grow several yards long if not pruned, has thick, rigid leaves to about 4 inches long and half as wide, and produces big, round clusters of pinkish-white flowers that are fragrant and appear to be made of wax. Can be trained on a pillar. 'Variegata' has white edges with a touch of pink; 'Exotica' has yellow and pink variegation. *Hoya carnosa compacta* 'Hindu Rope' has tightly curled leaves.

Yesterday, Today, and Tomorrow
Brunfelsia pauciflora

Though hardy outdoors in most coastal areas, this small shrubby perennial looks bad for awhile in the fall and winter. Growing it in a pot makes it easier to prune to keep it within bounds, and to move it around or out of sight. It also brings its flowers (which fade from purple to lavender to white—hence it's folksy common name) closer for viewing. 'Macrantha' has fewer but much larger flowers.

Truck Crop in a Bag

Being a garden radio host and newspaper columnist puts me in direct contact with "real gardeners" who often tell it like it is. But I once lost patience with a fella who was whining about not being able to garden. Too busy, he said. Or was it too tired or just plain lazy? No matter. He just didn't think he could do it.

But I believe that anyone can garden. I mean, even the Bird Man of Alcatraz found a way to have a hobby, right? So I set up the simplest possible kind of garden, in the toughest imaginable spot: The bed of my pickup truck.

I took a plain bag of ordinary potting soil, cut some X slits in the top, poked in a little timed-release fertilizer, and stuck in a pepper plant, a tomato plant, and a Madagascar periwinkle plant—all sun-loving and heat-tolerant. I set the "pillow garden" up close to the cab of my truck where the wind wouldn't buffet it as much, called it my "truck crop" and kept it alive—and producing—the entire summer.

When I stopped for gas, I'd water the plants. When whiteflies and aphids attacked, I headed for the freeway and drove really fast (worked like a charm).

There are better places to have a little garden, and of course a myriad of containers—plastic, clay, home-made hypertuffa, wood (including recycled wine barrels), pots, pans, boots, bathtubs, or even tires (to which I am partial). Mostly it needs to hold up to weather and watering, and have a drainage hole.

Point is, anybody can have a garden, anywhere. In fact, if anyone thinks they can do better than growing flowers and veggies in the back of a pickup, I say go for it. Yoda, who during *Star Wars* said "Do or do not—there is no try," would have been too mature to tell that lazy fella what I did on the radio: Stop whining!

Perennials
THAT PREVAIL

Perennials—generally herbaceous plants that live three or more years—are "hot" in California gardens, partly because many of them grow with little care, and partly because the nursery and landscape industry has started promoting them more.

Unfortunately, many popular perennial plants from other parts of the country—peonies and astilbe come to mind—simply cannot survive out West. On the other hand, Californians can easily grow astounding tropical, subtropical, and Mediterranean perennials that have to be treated as potted plants elsewhere. It's a good swap, and this chapter highlights a few dozen of the very best adapted for California's climate.

Site Selection and Soil Preparation

Although some perennials, such as ferns and gingers, tolerate heavy shade, many others bloom best with at least half a day of sunshine. Both good soil drainage and air circulation—and not over watering—are very important for avoiding root and foliage diseases. Soil preparation for perennials is similar to that for annuals, but do it well the first time, because perennials may grow for years with little opportunity for you to correct any problems.

It is easier to get some plants started in soil that has been lightly amended with a little organic matter such as bark, peat, or compost (or a combination). This can help temporarily with drainage and hold nutrients during rainy spells, and hold

Kangaroo Paws

moisture between waterings in dry seasons. A layer of organic matter 2 or 3 inches deep, worked into the soil a shovel's depth, is usually adequate, and "feeds" the soil as it decomposes. NOTE: Some of our best, "toughest" perennials do better with NO soil amendments—a good mulch is much better in the long run.

Jupiter's Beard

Planting and Care

Set perennial plants level with or slightly higher than the soil around them, and completely cover roots without burying the stem or crown. Water thoroughly to settle the soil. Then mulch the bed surface to keep the soil from drying, crusting, and overheating in the summer and to prevent many weed seeds from germinating. Working up the soil surface in the spring to break and aerate compacted soils may help water penetration, but also brings weed seeds to the surface. Better to just use mulch.

Perennials need a balance of several nutrients; most garden supply stores carry a wide variety of fertilizer mixes. Slow-acting kinds are easier to use and better for plants than fast-acting liquids or generic garden fertilizers. Apply fertilizers sparingly to plants early in their growing season, after new growth begins to show. If plants are growing well, no additional fertilizer may be needed; otherwise, a second light feeding will be helpful several weeks into the season. The main thing to remember on feeding perennials is that a little is better than a lot, and too much is worse than none at all.

Propagation

Most gardeners find that digging and separating plants, each with its own piece of stem and roots, takes very little expertise; practice on a daylily or liriope for experience, and before long you will have the hang of it. Though

some perennials can be divided any time you feel like it, in general it is best to do it during their dormant or "off" season; divide spring bloomers in the fall and fall bloomers in spring. Usually the worst time is when they are in full bloom.

Quite a few perennial plants can be rooted from stem cuttings, choosing stems that are mature and firm but not yet hardened and woody. Cut off 4- to 6-inch segments, pinch off the succulent tip and any flower buds, and remove lower leaves that will be below the surface of the medium. Root in pots of a porous, well-drained rooting medium, such as a one-to-one mixture of sand, perlite, and peat moss, watering daily or as needed. Rooting usually happens within three or four weeks.

Combining Perennials and Other Plants

Make sure all plants in the same area have the same basic soil, sun, and watering needs. For best effect, contrast plants by foliage shape or color, or a simple, bold combination of "spiky" plants, "roundy" plants, and "frilly" plants. If needed, add a hard feature such as statue, birdbath, bench, or artwork to create a year-round scene.

Take a little extra care in choosing and planting perennials well, followed with mulch and occasional feeding and watering, and their lives and performance will be greatly extended.

 ## Best for Beginners:

- Artemisia
- Copper Canyon Daisy
- Daylily
- Fortnight Lily
- Iris
- Lily-of-the-Nile
- Liriope
- Society Garlic
- Yarrow

Kinda Tricky:

- Delphinium
- Heaths and Heathers
- Hellebore
- Hibiscus
- Lavender
- Lupine
- Potentilla
- Primrose

Agapanthus

Agapanthus species

Sun, part sun, part shade

The lily-of-the-Nile is one of the most commonly planted perennials across California, most often used as a border or in accent groups, massed as a groundcover, or in pots.

FLOWER: Large round clusters of dozens of funnel-shaped white, pale blue to deep violet-blue flowers on bare stems from 2 to 4 or more feet tall. Choose plants when in bloom to get what you want.

PLANT: Fountain-like clumps 2 or 3 three tall and wide of glossy, strap-like leaves spread slowly and rarely need dividing. Extremely drought tolerant.

INTERESTING KINDS: 'Elaine' has large clusters of purple-blue on 4-foot stems; 'Midnight Blue' has the deepest blue flowers; 'Tinkerbell' is a charming dwarf plant with medium blue flowers and leaves edged in cream; *A. praecox* 'Flore Pleno' has double flowers.

Artemisia

Artemisia species

Sun or light shade

One of the first plants introduced to the New World for its medicinal uses, various "wormwoods" and other sagebrush relatives have become landscape staples as durable, usually silvery-gray fillers in mixed borders, and groundcovers for dry shade and banks.

FLOWER: Insignificant, usually yellow.

PLANT: Billowy or ferny foliage, generally silvery gray or nearly white, can be cut in the spring to remove woody growth and stimulate soft new foliage. Most have a pungent smell when cut or bruised.

INTERESTING KINDS: 'Powis Castle' is one of the most universally planted for its cloud of gray, ferny foliage; 'Huntington' is similar, but with larger, softer leaves; upright 'Silver King' is not used much because of invasive runners, but is light and airy, and can be used in flower arrangements.

Bear's Breech
Acanthus mollis
Sun or shade

Classic, bold Mediterranean plant that needs plenty of room whether massed or used as a strong accent, especially when highlighted against a wall or evergreen shrubs.

FLOWER: Tall spires of white, rose, or purple flowers are partially hidden beneath spiny purplish or green bracts, often cut off by gardeners after they begin to fade.

PLANT: Spreading clump of large, deeply lobed leaves, sometimes spiny, usually around 2 feet across, for sun or shade; during prolonged dry spells the leaves can lose their green color or drop leaves, but can be revived with a good soaking.

INTERESTING KINDS: Latifolius hybrids have larger leaves than the species and are hardier; leaves of A. *spinosus* are more finely cut with a silvery cast; spinosissimus hybrids have bright green leaves.

California Fuchsia
Zauschneria californica
Sun

Very informal Western native with heat-resistant foliage and hot flowers, grown as unusual small accents, usually as filler beside boulders or other hard features where it can spread a little and its airy form will still be effective. This outstanding hummingbird magnet is also used as a ground-cover in dry naturalistic gardens.

FLOWER: Narrow trumpets of brilliant scarlet red or bright orange in summer and fall.

PLANT: Spreading, shrub-like evergreen with narrow, gray or silvery white leaves, very heat- and drought-tolerant. Can be sheared to thicken up its form, best done after flowering.

INTERESTING KINDS: Numerous cultivated varieties are available, including mound-like 'Clover Dale', compact 'Dublin', and pink-flowered 'Solidarity Pink'. 'Bowman' is an upright form.

Calla

Zantedeschia aethiopica

Part sun or part shade

This old pass-along plant is the only ground-hardy evergreen calla for most of California, and even gets a little weedy in wet areas (like under a dripping air conditioner, for example).

FLOWER: Artificial-looking white or creamy spathes up to 8 inches long are held slightly above foliage, wrapped around a single yellow finger-like spike (spadix). Flowers mostly in the spring, but under good conditions can continue into summer.

PLANT: Spreading clump of thin arrowhead shaped green leaves up to 4 feet tall, not spotted like tropical kinds. Needs shade in hot areas.

INTERESTING KINDS: 'Green Goddess' has large green-tipped flowers; 'Hercules' is the largest, with big white flowers that open flat and curve backwards. Miniature types (good for containers) include 'Minor' and 'Childsiana'.

Cast Iron Plant

Aspidistra elatior

Dense to part shade

The common name says it all—this old-garden plant, hardy enough to grow under live oaks, is a mainstay of shaded gardens; it can sunscald even in winter sun. It is an outstanding container plant on a shaded porch or patio.

FLOWER: Insignificant lilac or greenish-brown bell-shaped flowers are borne on very short stems at ground level in the spring, hidden by tall foliage.

PLANT: Pointed spearheads of deep, forest-green leaves to 2 or 3 feet tall and 4 inches or more wide, arise once a year in the late winter and early spring from clumps of roots and persist until the following year

INTERESTING KINDS: 'Variegata' has irregular-width streaks of pale yellow; 'Milky Way' has lots of white spots on green leaves.

Copper Canyon Daisy
Tagetes lemmonii
Sun

What's that smell? The leaves of this perennial marigold give off a pungent odor—not bad, really, just strong—even in a stiff breeze, but the big, airy plants flower all summer, with a knock-out show in late fall and into winter.

FLOWER: Single, golden orange blooms produced loosely at ends of thin branches are shown off well against a wall or evergreen hedge.

PLANT: Bushy with many lanky stems and finely-divided leaves, the 4 to 6 foot perennial can be easily pruned when it eventually gets too leggy or burned by frost. Can be grown as a fast-flowering annual as well.

INTERESTING KINDS: Closely related to Mexican mint marigold (*T. lucida*), which also flowers in late fall.

Cranesbill Geranium
Geranium species
Sun or afternoon shade

True geraniums are not quite as showy as the gaudy, thick pelargoniums we "call" geraniums, but they are dependable with little or no care.

FLOWER: Slender stems carry a scattering of five-petalled flowers in pink, white, magenta, purple, or blue, often with darker veins, from late spring to fall. Seedpods look like a beak (hence the common name). Some reseed prolifically (even to the point of being weedy).

PLANT: Upright or trailing plants with rounded, lobed, or deeply cut foliage from dark green to chartreuse, soft gray or glossy.

INTERESTING KINDS: 'Cambridge' is an outstanding groundcover with dark leaves and bluish pink flowers; 'Ballerina' has soft gray-green leaves and many pale pink flowers with dark veins. 'Wargrave Pink', 'Johnson's Blue', 'Brookside' and many other great selections are available.

Daylily
Hemerocallis species and hybrids
Full sun or light shade

It has been said that "wherever the sun shines, there is a daylily." These most eagerly grown perennials are mainstays of the summer flower garden. Find tips on growing and hybridizing daylilies, plus growers near you, through the American Hemerocallis Society (www.daylilies.org).

FLOWER: Large, six-petalled flowers from 3 to over 6 inches across, borne on sturdy stems from 6 inches to 6 feet tall. Colors range from pale yellow to blackish red, with everything in between except for pure white and pure blue, and flowers can be single colors or have contrasting "eyes" and throats, bicolor, banded, tipped, or edged. Flowers are edible, and can be served any way broccoli is used.

PLANT: Many flattened fans of long, slender, grass-like leaves grow from a central crown into clumps 1 to 3 feet tall and wide. Rust disease seems to be worse on over-fed, over-watered plants.

INTERESTING KINDS: With over 20,000 named cultivars, there are way too many "best" daylilies to mention here. My current favorites are small, long-blooming kinds used in borders or as mass plantings, including 'Stella d'Oro', 'Happy Returns,' and 'Pardon Me'. There are more even better ones coming out every year.

THE SINGLE MOST RECOGNIZABLE DAYLILY (*Hemerocallis fulva*), the old orange one seen growing along ditches, beside country homes, and in cemeteries—and even found in famous botanical gardens—is despised by "society" daylily growers because of its very commonness. Yet it and the double-flowering variety 'Kwanso', continue to be popular with new and cottage gardeners alike. They do not cause other daylilies to "revert" to the orange species form, but can spread from runners to crowd out less vigorous daylilies.

Dusty Miller
Several genera and species
Sun or light shade

Stick with me on this: No two gardeners will ever agree on what a dusty miller plant is, because there are any number of soft, white-foliage perennials and annuals called by that descriptive common name.

FLOWER: Usually airy summer stems with sprays of rounded flowers in white, yellow, or purple.

PLANT: Drought-resistant clumps or small shrubby perennials with soft divided leaves of gray, silvery gray, or white.

INTERESTING KINDS: *Centaurea cineraria*, a small clump-forming plant with velvety-white, strap-shaped leaves and purple or yellow summer blooms; *C. gymnocarpa* has more finely divided, felt-like foliage and purple summer flowers. *Senecio cineraria* is a 2-foot shrubby perennial with wooly white cut leaves with bluntly rounded lobes and yellow flowers nearly all season; *S. viravira* has strikingly white, deeply divided foliage and creamy white summer flowers. *Tanacetum ptarmiciflorum* is a tender perennial mum with finely cut, silvery-white leaves and white summer daisies. Also, some artemisias are called dusty miller, as is rose campion (*Lychnis coronaria*).

Euphorbia
Euphorbia characias ssp. *wulfenii*
Sun or part shade

Too bad there isn't a decent common name for this uncommonly bold plant, which is in the same family as crown of thorns, pencil cactus, snow-on-the-mountain, and poinsettia. But the no-name spurge is still a great plant—in fact, it can get out of hand with seedlings.

FLOWER: Stalks topped with large cylindrical or round clusters of lime green flowers from spring to summer, that hold their color for many weeks. When using for bouquets, burn the cut end to seal in sap.

PLANT: Multiple-stemmed perennial to 4 or 5 feet tall and wide, each stem tightly packed with narrow green or blue-green leaves. Very drought tolerant. Milky sap may irritate the skin of some gardeners.

INTERESTING KINDS: *Euphorbia characias* ssp. *characias* 'Humpty Dumpty' is only about 2 feet tall and wide.

Ferns
All sorts of weird Latin names
Shade or part shade

Holly Fern

Ferns bring a primordial mystery to the garden, whether
used as textured accents or as lush groundcovers. They complement woodland shrubs, act as skirts
for leggy trees, mark paths, or tone down benches or other "hard" features. There are a great many
good ferns for California gardens, including natives and exotics, but here is a good start with a
few that have proven tough enough to survive on their own in woodsy, partly shaded gardens for
years to come. Staghorn fern (*Platycerium bifurcatum*) is discussed in the Patio Plants chapter.

Chain Fern (*Woodwardia fimbriata*) is a huge native fern, found growing naturally from Mexico
to British Columbia. Woody rhizomes creep through mulch and send up thick, leathery fronds to
4 to 5 feet tall (nearly twice that tall in moist coastal forests). This fern can grow in desert areas
if planted in moist, shaded areas. Once established they are little or no maintenance.

Deer Fern (*Blechnum spicant*) is a tidy plant, native to coastal
forests, that has two different kinds of fronds: Sterile fronds are over
2 feet long but less than 2 inches wide and spread outward from the
clump; fertile fronds grow straight up and are more slender, with
widely spaced leaflets.

Holly Fern (*Cyrtomium falcatum*) is the best evergreen fern for
shaded areas, forming a 2 to 3 foot tall and wide, "bird's nest" rosette
of stiff fronds, with many slick, dark green leaflets, each up to
3 inches wide and long like a holly leaf. Requires shade, even in the
winter under deciduous trees.

Japanese Painted Fern (*Athyrium nipponicum* 'Pictum') is an
evergreen clump to 18 inches tall, with lower portions of each
arrowhead shaped frond having purplish leaflets, gradually
lightening towards the top in shades of lavender to silvery green; it
is a little fussy and needs good soil and water.

Deer Fern

Southern Sword Fern (*Nephrolepis cordifolia*) grows 2 to 3 feet tall,
but spreads twice that wide. Fronds are bright green and narrow—like its close relative, the
tropical Boston fern—and the plant makes a good groundcover as it spreads rapidly in moist
soils. Will grow in the sun if watered regularly.

Western Sword Fern (*Polystichum munitum*) is a native forest plant, 3 to 4 feet high and
wide, with erect, leathery fronds that are shiny and dark. Each leaflet is like a short sword
and hilt. Established plants need very little attention.

Propagate ferns while they are dormant or nearly so in the winter. To keep from losing them, cut
off all or most of the fronds (they will grow back) and move only the shallow rhizomes and roots,
getting plenty of the native soil with them. Plant immediately and water thoroughly. Tough,
attractive new growth should come up quickly, so you won't be fern-less for long.

Fortnight Lily or African Iris
Dietes species
Sun or light shade

Talk about tough—this iris relative can grow and bloom in cracks in the concrete between sidewalks and parking lots!

FLOWER: Waxy iris flowers can be white, cream, or yellow, with contrasting blotches on each of the three outer petals. Each stiff flowering stem can produce for many months; don't cut them until they are completely spent.

PLANT: Thick evergreen stands of sword-like iris foliage 2 to 3 feet tall, tolerant of every kind of soil and moisture. Divide only when you need more plants.

INTERESTING KINDS: *Dietes grandiflora* 'Johnsonii' is over 3 feet tall with white flowers blotched in brown and yellow that stay open three days without closing. Hybrid 'Lemon Drops' has lemon yellow blotches; 'Orange Drops' has orange blotches.

Four O'Clocks
Mirabilis jalapa
Sun or light shade

The "Japanese Miracle Flower" of today's garden shows, is the same "Marvel of Peru" of Thomas Jefferson's day, and it continues to rapidly spread around the world, one garden at a time.

FLOWER: Intensely fragrant small trumpets of white, yellow, pink, or hot magenta open late in the day, followed by pea-size seeds that can sprout within days into almost-flowering new plants.

PLANT: This shrubby perennial with pointed oval green leaves returns dependably every spring from a large, rough tuberous root.

INTERESTING KINDS: 'Broken Colors' and the Jingles strain have streaks and flecks of several colors on each flower (Jingles are also smaller than the species); 'Golden Sparkles' is yellow tipped with pink; 'Baywatch' is a large plant with pale yellow flowers.

Gaura
Gaura lindheimeri
Sun

A surprisingly tough eastern prairie native, this airy perennial has nearly constant flower production, and is just as constantly loaded with butterflies. Excellent as a filler in sunny, dry flower borders.

FLOWER: Long, gently arching stems to 3 or 4 feet tall are studded with pink buds that open into inch-long flowers of pink or white. Deadheading will increase the number of new flowers, and reduce its tendency to reseed everywhere.

PLANT: Clump forming with many thin branches and thin leaves. Deep taproot increases it drought tolerance. No need to divide, just move seedlings.

INTERESTING KINDS: Cultivars are more mannerly than the species. 'Whirling Butterflies' has larger white flowers; 'Siskiyou Pink' has deep maroon buds that open to rose pink flowers, and leaves mottled with maroon.

Gazania
Gazania hybrids
Sun

This is my first choice for a big-flowered, long-blooming, low-growing plant in both flower beds and parking lot dividers, good soil or bad dirt, water or none.

FLOWER: Four-inch daisies come in a dazzling array of single colors or sunbursts with dark centers. Flowers appear spring to fall and through mild winters, but open only when the sun is bright, closing at night and on foggy days.

PLANT: Low-growing clump or fast-spreading trailing forms have green or gray leaves that tolerate heat and drought even in poor, dry soil.

INTERESTING KINDS: Clump-forming or spreading hybrids are available as both transplants and quick-to-bloom seeds. 'Fiesta Red' and 'Copper King' are extra sturdy; 'Moonglow' is double-flowering, bright yellow, and stays open on overcast days.

Geranium

Pelargonium × *hortorum*

Part sun or light shade

Longtime favorites from grandmother's garden, these long-blooming perennials with spicy-scented leaves are almost like little shrubs—and they can suffer from too much care.

FLOWER: Stiff stems topped with clusters of single or double flowers in red, white, pink, orange, and violet. Cut faded stems to encourage new flowers.

PLANT: Almost woody lower stems support succulent flowering stems with many large, kidney-shaped or roundish scalloped leaves that are softly fuzzy and fragrant when crushed or clipped. Foliage of most is dark green with a burgundy or maroon band inside the edge, but hybrids can have borders or splashes of orange, green, pink, rose, or violet.

INTERESTING KINDS: Heat-tolerant strains less likely to shut down during high summer include Orbit, Maverick, Americana, and Eclipse.

Goldenrod

Solidago species

Sun or very light shade

This seriously under-used autumn-blooming sunflower relative is unfairly blamed for allergies, of which it is totally innocent (wind-blown pollen from grasses and ragweed is the usual real culprit).

FLOWER: Very showy clusters of small, bright golden-yellow flowers form atop long, stiff stems in late summer and fall, and are outstanding as long-lasting cut flowers. Butterflies and bees flock to its non-allergenic pollen.

PLANT: Low-growing rosette with tall, usually non-branching stems with narrow leaves. Some species spread rapidly, others are tidy clump formers.

INTERESTING KINDS: Sweet goldenrod (*S. odora*) is tall, unbranched, and non-invasive, and has anise-scented leaves; rough-leaf goldenrod (*S. rugosa* 'Fireworks') has arching stems to 4 feet tall; *S. sphacelata* 'Golden Fleece' and hybrid 'Cloth of Gold' are under 2 feet tall.

Hellebore

Helleborus species

Shade or filtered sun

Hellebores are winter bloomers, with good summer foliage as well.

FLOWER: Downward-nodding cup or bell-shaped flowers up to 2 inches across on foot-tall cut-flower quality branched stems gradually dry and fade to green from their original white or pale green, pink, yellow, red, burgundy, or purple. Some have contrasting stripes or interesting spots.

PLANT: Slow-spreading clumps of finger-like leathery leaflets on foot-long stalks can live for decades.

INTERESTING KINDS: Leaves of Majorcan hellebore (*H. lividus*) are purple underneath, striped above with pale green tinged with purple; Corsican hellebore (*H. argutifolius*) 'Pacific Frost' is heat- and sun-tolerant even in Southern California, with white-marbled leaves; the Stern hybrids (*H. × sternii*) offer several colors from which to choose.

Hyssop-Mint

Agastache species and hybrids

Sun or part shade

These multiple-use North American natives and their hybrids tolerate all sorts of weather (especially heat), have aromatic leaves, a spiky form to complement any flower bed, and colorful flowers that are fantastic hummingbird attracters.

FLOWER: Dense clusters of mint-like flowers in a multitude of colors (depending on kind) on erect spires above foliage in summer can rebloom if old flower spikes are cut off.

PLANT: Narrow shrublike perennial around 1 to 3 feet tall with pointy-oval leaves that give off a pleasant herby fragrance when bruised.

INTERESTING KINDS: Hybrids include 'Blue Fortune' with light blue flowers; 'Firebird' with dark orange flowers; 'Tangerine Dreams' with large, deep orange flowers; and ' Summer Breeze' with dark, almost gray-green leaves and lavender-pink flowers.

Iris

Iris species and hybrids

Sun

Many irises are Old World perennials, with modern hybrids that produce dazzling flowers. Yet old standards can be found blooming faithfully beside long-abandoned homesteads. Their year-round foliage complements other plants.

FLOWER: Exotic combination of three upright petals ("standards") and three cascading "falls" glow in literally every color of the rainbow. Some of the spring-bloomers repeat in late summer.

PLANT: Finger-like rhizomes sprout smooth, sword-like foliage from a few inches to several feet tall, attractive as garden texture even without flowers. Overwatering can rot rhizomes.

INTERESTING KINDS: Pacific Coast and Douglas (*I. douglasiana*) irises are sturdy natives that can easily outlive more refined hybrids with little or no attention. Showy orange seedpods of the very drought-tolerant Gladwin iris (*I. foetidissima*) are welcome in the fall garden, and in flower arrangements.

Jerusalem Sage

Phlomis species

Sun

This Mediterranean native is a non-stop attention-getter, with furry gray leaves and ball-shaped flower clusters, attractive even after flowering stems have dried.

FLOWER: Erect stems have evenly-spaced whorls of unusual hooded yellow, purple, or lilac flowers from spring to fall, very striking both in the garden and in flower arrangements.

PLANT: Spreading clump or upright "shrub," with many stems covered with usually gray or gray-green furry or hairy leaves.

INTERESTING KINDS: 'Edward Bowles' (also known as 'Lemon Swirls') is a hybrid with broad, hand-size leaves and large, pure yellow flowers. Other great species include compact *P. lanata*; *P. purpurea* with purplish-pink flowers; heart-leaved, groundcovering *P. russeliana* with soft yellow flowers; and *P. samia*, similar to the last but with purple flowers.

Jupiter's Beard
Centranthus ruber
Sun or shade

New gardeners are always surprised when more experienced hands describe this showy Mediterranean wildflower as "weedy" because it is simply so easy to grow without any human attention. Still, it is best to enjoy it in areas where you can keep an eye on its prolific seedlings.

FLOWER: Small flowers, usually red, crimson, or pale pink, are arranged into dense clusters on slightly branched stems above the plants in late spring and summer.

PLANT: Generic bushy clump under 3 feet high has bluish green leaves and tolerates any kind of growing condition, soil type, or moisture. They literally grow everywhere except in low, wet, shaded areas (of which there are few in California!).

INTERESTING KINDS: 'Albus' has white flowers.

Kangaroo Paws
Anigozanthos species and hybrids
Sun

This dramatic Australian native is hardy except where watered to death or where it can freeze. But even out of its perfect zone it can still be prized as a low-water container plant.

FLOWER: Irregular, arching spires up to 5 feet tall have loosely-arranged fuzzy, tubular flowers that bend a little at the tips, making them look like hairy kangaroo paws. If old flowering stems are removed, the plants can flower from spring to fall.

PLANT: Dark green sword-like leaves sprout from a thick, drought-tolerant rhizome that stores moisture so the plant can survive for weeks with no irrigation.

INTERESTING KINDS: 'Big Red' has large red flowers; 'Harmony' has yellow flowers on red-fuzzed stems; 'Pink Joey' blooms at 3 feet with pink flowers. Bush Gem hybrids are small and resistant to root rot.

Lavender
Lavandula species
Sun

Loved for their irresistibly fragrant flowers, aromatic foliage, butterflies and bees, and pure low maintenance, there are almost too many lavenders to settle on just one.

FLOWER: Fragrant spikes of violet, blue, lavender, burgundy, pink, or white from spring to fall, and through mild winters.

PLANTS: Spiky clumps of gray, yellow-green, or gray-green foliage require low water and low fertility, best used as edging, informal hedges, in herb or container gardens, or well-drained flower borders with good air circulation. NOTE: Seed-grown kinds are highly variable; always buy those grown from cuttings, or root your own.

INTERESTING KINDS: Super-hardy perennial types worth highlighting, with many good selections available in each, include sprawling "fernleaf" lavender (*L. multifida*); stocky Spanish lavender (*L. stoechas*); English lavender (*L. angustifolia*); shrubby French lavender (*L. dentata*); hybrid 'Goodwin Creek Grey' is densely leaved; and the large, heat- and humidity-tolerant *L. × intermedia*.

Liriope
Liriope muscari
Part sun

Don't take this versatile border plant for granted—use it as an accent, a durable companion to less sturdy flowers, or as a tough container plant. Its flower spikes make good cut flowers.

FLOWER: Stiff summer spires shoot 6 to 12 inches above foliage, and are studded with purple, blue, pink, or white flowers.

PLANT: Sturdy grass-like clumps do not spread like creeping lilyturf (*L. spicata*); can be divided annually. Tough enough to be planted almost on top of the ground for a showier fountain-like effect.

INTERESTING KINDS: 'Variegata' is showy even in low-light sites, almost shining along paths at dusk; 'Majestic' (actually *L. exiliflora*) blooms heavily with thick spikes of dark violet; 'Silvery Sunproof' has gold stripes that turn white. 'Monroe White' has white flowers.

Matillija Poppy
Romneya coulteri
Sun

Called "fried egg flower" for good reason (see photo), this aggressive native is considered a big-time weed by some designers, who are heavily outnumbered by gardeners who prize it highly.

FLOWER: Huge, cut-flower quality blossoms have flat, crinkled petals around a golden-yellow center, produced from late spring into fall.

PLANT: Thick stems shooting up from spreading rhizomes are loosely covered with large gray-green, lobed leaves. Plant where it can be contained or it will take over nearby flower or shrub borders. Better yet, plant in large areas, hillsides, or behind moderate-size evergreen shrubs where its legginess will be concealed.

INTERESTING KINDS: 'Butterfly' branches heavily and is covered with many rounded flowers with overlapping petals. 'White Cloud' is very prolific with huge blossoms on a vigorous plant.

Mexican Petunia
Ruellia brittoniana
Sun

This native Mexican perennial, attractive as a non-stop butterfly and hummingbird garden plant, blooms best in warm or hot seasons.

FLOWER: Flaring, petunia-like trumpets of blue, pink, or white, 2 inches across, on spidery stems. Several dozen flowers per clump open every morning and last through the following night.

PLANT: Many upright stems, with pairs of narrow, dark-green leaves opposite one another in knobby nodes, shoot quickly to 3 or 4 feet tall (taller in the shade), and spread slowly but surely by seed and underground stems. Best suited to perennial borders where there is room to spread or in large containers or beside water gardens. Fast-rooting in water.

INTERESTING KINDS: 'Purple Showers' is sterile (non-seeding) and more free-flowering; 'Chi Chi' has pink flowers.

Penstemon
Penstemon hybrids
Sun

The group of hybrid beardtongues has many garden-quality varieties that grow well in the most populated areas of California including harsh urban environments.

FLOWER: Stiff stems of small trumpet-shaped reds, pinks, purples, salmon, and white, all designed for hummingbirds, and to be cut and put into vases. Mainly flower in the spring, but cutting faded stems jump-starts more flowers for fall.

PLANT: Narrow leaves on small shrubby plants that require very fast drainage—if nothing else, set plants on top of the ground and pile soil up to them.

INTERESTING KINDS: 'Apple Blossom', 'Garnet', 'Firebird', 'Midnight', and 'Holly's White' are all dependable and generally available.

Purple Heart
Tradescantia pallida
Sun or light shade

Intense conditions call for intense plants. The gaudy purple-red foliage of this nearly indestructible spreading plant belies its toughness—it grows just as well in traffic medians as in flower borders or containers. This heirloom is so easy to propagate, it all but spreads itself from garden to garden by way of easy-to-root "liberated" bits and pieces. It is a close relative to wandering Jew, but is bolder and much hardier.

FLOWER: Ends of runners produce fairly showy half-inch wide, clear pink flowers with three petals that stand out strongly against the backdrop of dark foliage.

PLANT: Spreading foot-tall mass of pointed, finger-like purple-red leaves that are squeaky slick to the touch.

INTERESTING KINDS: 'Purpurea' has stunning purple foliage.

Salvia
Salvia species
Sun or light shade

Violet Sage

All salvias are fantastic butterfly and hummingbird plants, and most make good cut flowers as well. Trouble is, there are so many kinds from which to choose; some do better than others in different parts of the state.

FLOWER: Generally long, tall spikes of blue, purple, white, or red, two-lipped trumpets either spaced singly above one another or packed densely into one solid spike of color. Most of the hardy salvias are summer flowering, some only in the short days of spring and fall.

PLANT: Spreading masses of stems bear slick, or sometimes grayish-white, velvety leaves up to 4 inches long and sometimes nearly as wide, often very fragrant (sage, the widely used culinary herb, is a hardy salvia). Counting the flower stalks, salvias can range from a foot or less tall and over 5 feet tall and wide. Pinching new growth of taller varieties makes them more compact, as will cutting them back lightly after they begin to fade from the first flush of blooms. Salvias need good air circulation to reduce mildew on leaves, and most will not tolerate staying wet. An occasional slow, deep soaking is much better than regular irrigation (some varieties need no more than one soaking a month).

Brazilian Sage (*S. guaranitica*) has wide leaves and 5-foot stems topped with spikes of deep or clear blue flowers that are loaded for hummingbirds; good cultivars include dark purplish 'Black and Blue' and pale blue 'Argentine Skies'.

Hybrid 'Indigo Spires' is large and sprawling but easily pruned into compact form, with narrow, twisted spikes of closely spaced violet-blue flowers during the entire warm season, and purple calyxes that persist after flowers are shed.

Bog Sage (*S. uliginosa*) is an airy plant to about 6 feet with narrow, fragrant leaves and spikes of pale blue and white flowers, but can be invasive in moist soils by underground runners.

Violet Sage (*S. nemorosa* and the similar *S. × superba*) is a spreading plant with narrow, erect flowering stems to nearly 3 feet tall covered with many violet-blue or purple flowers all summer; 'East Friesland' is one of the best cultivars.

Forsythia Sage (*S. madrensis*) has yellow-orange flowers and thick, four-sided stems up to 8 feet tall.

Sea Lavender or Statice
Limonium perezii
Sun

Some call it gaudy, some say it is weedy; everyone, from managers of botanic gardens to mobile home parks, agrees that it is showy.

FLOWER: Large, brilliant clusters nodding atop 3-foot stems are a combination of rich purple and white, from spring through fall. Note: Seedlings can invade sensitive natural areas.

PLANT: Clump-forming masses of deep green leaves that are a foot long and more than half that wide. Plants can tolerate beach and even hot roadside growing conditions, but are damaged by freezes down into the mid-twenties. Nursery-grown seedlings grow and bloom fast.

INTERESTING KINDS: The species can hardly be beat, especially when combined with gray-leaf companions. *Limonium platyphyllum* (*L. latifolium*) is smaller with smooth-edged leaves, and can be found with white forms.

Shasta Daisy
Leucanthemum × superbum
Sun or light shade

My first visit to pioneering horticulturist Luther Burbank's garden in Santa Rosa was humbling, but to see the stand of Shasta daisies for which Burbank is well-known worldwide, was a thrilling peek at garden history.

FLOWER: Basic white "daisy" with thin, usually white flowers radiating from a golden-yellow disk, with the composite flower 2 to 4 inches across. Some are double-flowered. Each branched stem, 2 to 4 feet tall, holds many flowers, which are excellent for cutting for arrangements.

PLANT: Slow-spreading basal clump of coarse, slightly toothed, leathery-green leaves that get smaller as they extend up the flowering stems.

INTERESTING KINDS: New strains include yellow-flowering varieties, but I still stick with old-fashioned white 'Alaska' and double-blooming 'Marconi' (though I do like compact 'Little Miss Muffet' and 'Snow Lady').

Society Garlic
Tulbaghia violacea
Sun or light shade

The oil from the aromatic leaves of this super-garlicky perennial can wash out of a potted plant to permanently stain a wood deck with a greasy spot. Better to use in-ground in groups, border plantings, or a groundcover. But still hold your nose when passing by.

FLOWER: Airy round balls of pink, white, or lilac flowers are held well above foliage on slender, 2-foot stalks in the spring, summer, and fall.

PLANT: Evergreen mound of slender, bluish-green leaves that thrive in harsh conditions that include drought and radiated heat from walls.

INTERESTING KINDS: 'Variegata' has a creamy stripe down the center of each leaf. 'Tricolor' has leaves with white edges, with a pinkish cast that intensifies in cool weather. 'Silver Lace' has leaves edged in white.

Sunflower
Helianthus species
Sun

You see them around country cottages and along rural highways. The annual species, *H. annuus*, is North America's most important native agricultural crop. Let sunflowers be put to use cheering up your own garden.

FLOWER: Round central disks with many "ray" flowers create 3- to 4-inch flowers, usually dozens per plant.

PLANT: Upright, with sparse leaves, some plants topping 10 feet high, others branching into head-high shrubby plants. The fall-blooming types make a nice fast screen.

INTERESTING KINDS: The 10-foot-tall, clear yellow flowering Maximillian sunflower (*H. maximiliani*) is tough enough for the high desert, clearly the most commonly grown; invasive, tuber-like roots of 7-foot Jerusalem artichoke (*H. tuberosus*) are sold in markets as edible "sunchoke."

Yarrow
Achillea species and hybrids
Sun

This heirloom flowering perennial was introduced by colonists to wrap cuts and wounds. It is now enjoyed purely for its large, flat flower heads and ferny foliage.

FLOWER: Small white, yellow, golden, pink, terra-cotta, cerise, or red flowers in flat clusters up to 4 or 5 inches across, atop sturdy stems from 2 to 3 or more feet tall

PLANT: Spreading clump up to a foot or more tall with aromatic evergreen, finely divided, soft leaves. Most spread aggressively, but don't cope well with excessive irrigation or high humidity. Plant in super-well-drained sites.

INTERESTING KINDS: Best cut-flower yarrows (mostly A. *filipendulina*) include 'Cloth of Gold'. Hybrids include yellow 'Coronation Gold' and 'Moonshine', golden 'Fireland' ('Feuerland'), mixed-color 'Anthea', and pink 'Appleblossom'. *Achillea millefolium* cultivars have the most fern-like leaves.

Other Good Perennials:

Buckwheats (*Eriogonum* species) are very tough natives with lots of small but showy clusters of flowers that grow well in gravelly soils and steep banks. St. Catherine's lace (*E. giganteum*) is showy even when not in bloom.

California Columbine (*Aquilegia formosa*) has good foliage and dependable, nodding red-and-yellow flowers, great in woodland gardens where it can self-seed itself around.

Coral Bells (*Heuchera* species and hybrids) have clumps of foliage, usually very colorful, variegated, or deep and dark, great for contrasting with other, finer-textured plants. Airy flowers add to the mystique. Many are native species or have native species in their parentage.

Ginger (*Asarum caudatum*) is a native woodland plant with glossy heart-shaped leaves, great in the Fog Belt as a shade groundcover.

Hardy Begonia (*Begonia grandis*) is a spreading, hardy evergreen (goes dormant and dies down in cold winters), a popular old "pass-along plant" with lopsided oval leaves of pale green with pinkish stems, and airy flowers of pink or white.

Hooker's Evening Primrose (*Oenothera elata* ssp. *hookeri*) is a low clump of lance-shaped leaves that sprout a continuous show of branching spikes with pale yellow to orange-red evening flowers. Tolerates both dry and wet spells, but not good for over-irrigated or mannerly gardens (it's a notorious re-seeder!).

Hyssop (*Hyssopus officinalis*) is very similar in landscape use as lavender. Compact to about 2 feet by 3, with lots of dark blue flower spikes through the summer, with white, pink or lavender kinds sometimes offered for sale. Edible leaves are pungent and peppery.

Kahili Ginger (*Hedychium gardnerianum*), with long, wide leaves and yellow flowers with showy red stamen, and ginger lily (*H. coronarium*) with pure white, very fragrant flowers, are root-hardy tropicals even in freeze-prone areas. Grow best in moist soil. Variegated ginger (*Alpinia*) is not freeze-tolerant.

Plume Poppy (*Macleaya cordata*) is a spreading, somewhat invasive clump of 5- to 8-foot stems clothed with large, deeply-lobed, tropical-looking leaves, topped with thick, feathery sprays of small off-white summer flowers. While Mexican species are less hardy, *M. microcarpa* 'Coral Plume' has pink flowers.

Red Hot Poker (*Kniphofia* species) is an unruly clump of grassy foliage topped with stunning spires tightly packed with narrow tubular flowers of mostly yellows, reds, or oranges that bloom from the bottom up and often change colors as they mature. Needs good moisture when forming flowers.

Santa Barbara Daisy (*Erigeron karvinskianus*) is a trailing, somewhat invasive native that practically never stops blooming with dozens of dainty lavender daisies. Well-adjusted to rock gardens, large containers, dry rock walls, or as a groundcover in dry flower beds.

Plume Poppy

Soapworts (*Saponaria* species) are sprawling plants with slick leaves (crushed foliage and roots of "bouncing bet", *S. officinalis*, were used for soap-making), with pink or white spring and summer flowers; they have been seen growing along railroad tracks.

Stokes' Aster (*Stokesia laevis*) is a native of the Southeast, with clumps of finger-shaped leaves (like fat liriope) and large clusters of outstanding frilly blue or white, sometimes yellow or pink, spring flowers. Needs water and can look ratty towards the end of a long season.

Verbena (*Verbena* species and hybrids) includes some outstanding species and cultivars, mostly spreading plants with ferny leaves and showy masses of flowers in the spring and summer. Most need water, or do best in natural areas where they can fade without notice during part of the season.

Verbena

141

Green Thumb Is Official

The "green thumb" has been officially declared a type of intelligence!

As a horticulturist, I was taught that it's all about positive human qualities such as the ability to be observant, pay attention to detail, plan ahead, and follow through on projects. But you know there's just gotta be something different, if not outright special, about folks who seem to be blessed with an unfair advantage in the natural world.

At last, Harvard professor Howard Gardner proved his "Theory of Multiple Intelligences" by finding regions of the brain that "light up" when certain abilities are practiced. In addition to the most widely accepted logical-mathematical, musical, and language-oriented "linguistics" aptitudes, he also found evidence of six other types of intelligences.

The one that most applies to the kind of gardener who can root and grow a splinter off a fencepost is called naturalist intelligence. Simply put, people with naturalist intelligence have the ability to identify and classify patterns in nature and make predictions based on seemingly random events.

Naturalists are very comfortable outdoors; they are constantly aware of their surroundings, looking around as they drive, watching weeds and hawks, and braking for butterflies. They observe, touch, and compare even "yucky" things, and often collect stuff—shells, rocks, and flowers. They can "just tell" when to plant, when to harvest, when to repot, when to water.

They also manipulate things to see what happens; ever-curious plant hybridizers fall heavily into the naturalists, as do "giant tomato" or "perfect lawn" gardeners. So do wildflower enthusiasts, bonsai artists, bird watchers, and garden teachers, especially those whose naturalist leanings are coupled with strong interpersonal and linguistic abilities.

Any of this apply to you? Mix in doses of other intelligences, and it's no wonder gardeners have such different approaches, and levels of success and satisfaction. We may not all be smart in the decisions we make—but a Harvard professor has proven that we can sure be intelligent in how we garden!

STEADFAST
Shrubs

Want to really have a low-maintenance landscape that looks good every month of the year? Your choice of shrubs, and how they are planted that very first time, can make or break the landscape.

Along with trees, vines, and palms, long-lived woody shrubs create the basic framework around which other flowers revolve. They are the "bones" of the garden, providing year-round focal points, lines, hedges, masses, and security. Plus, when compared with annuals and perennials, and especially the lawn, these long-lived plants are generally as close to low maintenance as anything you can grow.

This chapter is packed with great selections, each "signed off on" by some of California's top garden experts as being beautiful, useful, tough enough to be fairly low maintenance, and still give a special "sense of place" unique to California. There are many other good plant choices, but these keep rising to the top of the heap for durability and beauty, and include even some of the native and "edgier" ones that many garden designers turn away from as "common" (hey —they *work!*).

Not-So Secrets for Success

Getting shrubs started for the long haul is easy, if you follow these

Hollywood Junipers

simple tips: Choose good plants, place them in appropriate conditions (sun or shade, wet soil or dry), dig or prepare a wide hole if you can, and loosen the roots when planting. Adding soil amendments to your native soil is an outdated practice that is being recommended less and less, especially with tough plants. Mulches, deep soakings, and light feedings can help get plants established so well they will survive—even thrive—for decades with little or no attention. Really. Oh, and if your underlying soil is mucky, clay, or rocky, raise the area with something similar to what is already there so plants don't have to get used to two different kinds of soil.

Year-Round Texture Is Easy

Keeping in mind the ideal textural combination of "spiky, roundy, and frilly," you can have an interesting twelve-month landscape by combining several kinds of shrubs with contrasting forms and foliage. My favorites include the bright green, teardrop-shaped arborvitae contrasted perfectly with the burgundy winter foliage of heavenly bamboo (*Nandina*); throw in a rosemary, and an airy, tree-form manzanita, and you'll have an eye-catching combo! Crape myrtles, Indian hawthorn, or althaea look even better when underplanted with groundcover junipers, artemisia, or ice plant. Mix and match at a garden center to see what works for you.

Birds Love Shrubs

Not only do shrubs provide texture, flowers, and fragrance for our gardens, they also make terrific perching, feeding, and nesting sites for native birds. Anything evergreen or with berries is a plus, but the real key to providing good wildlife habitat is *diversity*—special attention needs to be given to planting something for all seasons, because, after all, our native wildlife is out there all year, not just in the seasons convenient to humans.

Shrubs with good bird fruits include holly, pyracantha, coffeeberry, ligustrum, and prickly pear cactus. Examples of good shrubs that provide cover include arborvitae, bottlebrush, California lilac, hollies, and ligustrum. There are many others, of course.

Bottle Tree

Silica transparencii

Sun or shade

Whether glistening in the sun or drawing good feng shui light into a dim area, this colorful, whimsical creation, which has roots in ancient history, is the absolute lowest maintenance, drought-hardy addition to any garden.

FLOWER: Small to medium glass cylinders of clear, amber, green, blue, and occasionally a rare red. Found on the ends of stems. "Blooms" all year.

PLANT: Upright, narrow or sprawling bare limbs rooted firmly in a hole in the ground, or tied to a fence post for better wind tolerance. Place where people of good cheer can have their day brightened.

INTERESTING KINDS: Cobalt blue, beer bottle brown, or Napa Valley wine jug green. Available in single colors or mixed (*S. transparencii* 'Kaleidoscope Stroke').

👍 Best for Beginners:

- Arborvitae
- Ceanothus
- Firethorn
- Flowering Quince
- Holly
- Juniper
- Lavender
- Manzanita
- Pomegranate
- Rosemary

Kinda Tricky: 👎

- Boxwood (pruning)
- Buddleja
- Camellia (needs rich soil)
- Hydrangea
- Lemonade Berry (hard to find)
- Oleander (new pests)

Abelia
Abelia × grandiflora
Sun or shade

This long-blooming favorite of hummingbirds, butterflies, and moths can be sheared tightly or allowed to grow informally.

FLOWER: Clusters of small white to pink tubular bells, spring through fall, surrounded with pink sepals that persist after the flowers fall off, almost like small pink blossoms.

PLANT: Evergreen shrub, 3 to 6 tall and wide, with graceful arching branches covered with small glossy, pointed oval leaves of green with a bronze cast in the fall.

INTERESTING KINDS: 'Francis Mason' is compact and dense with pink flowers and variegated leaves; 'Golden Glow' has yellow foliage; 'Prostrata' makes a dependable groundcover for slopes. Hybrid 'Edward Goucher' is dwarf, airy, and pink flowering. Chinese abelia (*A. chinensis*) has large, thick clusters of flowers, worth seeking out if not available locally.

Arborvitae
Thuja occidentalis orientalis
Full sun or part shade

The "tree of life" is an old standby tough enough for cemetery conditions. Its brilliant color and dependable shape make it indispensable for garden "oomph."

FLOWER: No "flowers," just interesting small, bumpy round blue cones in winter.

PLANT: Teardrop, round, or irregular shrubs of dense emerald or golden frond-like fans of tiny scale-like leaves.

INTERESTING KINDS: 'Emerald' is a dense, narrow cone to about 15 feet tall and 4 feet wide; 'Globosa' remains tightly rounded to about 3 feet ('Little Gem' and 'Little Giant' are similar); 'Rheingold' is cone-shaped, slow-growing, and bright golden, only 4 or 5 feet tall; 'Woodwardii' is an old-fashioned globular arborvitae that grows very slowly up to around 8 feet. 'Degroot's Spire' and 'Brabant' are narrow and columnar.

Aucuba
Aucuba japonica
Shade

Hard to beat as a dense evergreen in the shade, Aucuba competes well with tree roots and tolerates sea air. Variegated forms can bring good *feng shui* as they brighten dark areas.

FLOWER: Insignificant maroon flowers in early spring, but when both male and female varieties are set near one another, $3/4$-inch bright red berries will form on the females.

PLANT: Evergreen with hand-size glossy green leaves, sometimes blotched or splashed with golden yellow, on shrubs that can get 6 to 10 feet tall and wide.

INTERESTING KINDS: 'Picturata' has a golden center blotch; 'Sulphurea Marginata' has a yellow edge to each leaf; 'Variegata' is splashed with yellow spots; 'Fructu Albo' has white markings.

Blue Puya
Puya species
Sun

This Chilean native, a spiky mass of cool teal blue, is one of the largest hardy bromeliads.

FLOWER: Flower stalks up to 6 feet tall look like giant asparagus spears before opening with clusters of blue-green bell-shaped blossoms with bright orange flower parts.

PLANT: Large gray-green clump of many sharp, sword-like leaves with spiny edges. Grows in poor but well-drained soil. Dramatic on slopes or banks, especially with large rocks or boulders. Also good with cacti and succulents, or in large contrasting-color containers.

Blue Sotol
Dasylirion wheeleri
Sun

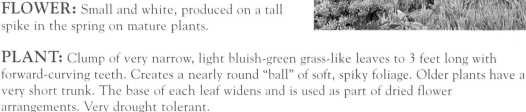

This Mexican native grows in a round clump 4 feet tall and wide; very dramatic architecturally when grown in pots for added height.

FLOWER: Small and white, produced on a tall spike in the spring on mature plants.

PLANT: Clump of very narrow, light bluish-green grass-like leaves to 3 feet long with forward-curving teeth. Creates a nearly round "ball" of soft, spiky foliage. Older plants have a very short trunk. The base of each leaf widens and is used as part of dried flower arrangements. Very drought tolerant.

INTERESTING KINDS: 'Zaragosa Blue Twister' (*D. berlandieri*) is the bluest of the sotols, very hardy and fast growing with leaves that twist, and flower spikes of chartreuse (female) and rust (male) flowers. *Dasylirion texanum* is a green sotol.

Bottlebrush
Callistemon species
Sun

This signature Australian native shrub produces waves of new growth with fuzzy flowers that all but scream "hummingbird"—and for good reason.

FLOWER: Dense clusters of long, bristle-like flower parts of red or yellow are followed by long-lasting woody fruit capsules that look like beads.

PLANT: Evergreen leaves are long and thin, sometimes with coppery new growth, easy to prune to keep in bounds or to shape into a small tree or train against a wall or fence.

INTERESTING KINDS: Lemon bottlebrush (*C. citrinus*) is common, with lemony-scented foliage (when crushed); 'Compacta' lemon bottlebrush is a mere 4 or 5 feet tall and wide; 'Little John' is the most dwarf, and possibly the most floriferous; white bottlebrush (*C. salignus*) has pale yellow flowers; weeping bottlebrush (*C. viminalis*) has several variations including 'Captain Cook' and 'Little John'.

Boxwood
Buxus species
Sun or part shade

One of the most popular generic green shrubs for small hedges, boxwood will tolerate a lot of neglect, but performs better with minimal care. Some are intolerant of alkaline soils.

FLOWER: Insignificant, and no berries, but a good backdrop for something more colorful.

PLANT: Upright, roundish shrub with small fingernail-size leaves. Often used as a clipped hedge, it can still look full even when given less strict treatment.

INTERESTING KINDS: 'Green Beauty' is the best Japanese boxwood (*B. japonica*) for holding winter color; true dwarf boxwoods (*B. sempervirens* 'Suffruticosa' and 'Vardar Valley') are very hardy. A *superb alternative* to common boxwood for low hedges, narrow beds, and topiary is African boxwood (*Myrsine africana*), which has much stiffer leaves.

Bush Germander
Teucrium fruticans
Sun

This Mediterranean shrub, which tolerates or even thrives in poor, rocky soils and areas where irrigation is not overdone, is not planted often enough—in spite of how it can bloom almost year-round.

FLOWER: Spikes of lavender-blue flowers are continually produced on the ends of new growth.

PLANT: This somewhat airy or loose shrub has a grayish overall appearance because of silvery stems and thin, grayish leaves with dusty white undersides, which help it tolerate hot, dry conditions. The shrub can be pruned in late winter or early spring to produce thicker plants with more flowers.

INTERESTING KINDS: 'Azureum' has deep blue flowers; 'Compactum' has dark flowers but grows only 3 or 4 feet tall and wide.

Butterfly Bush
Buddleja species

Sun

Buddleja is very popular as an all-summer butterfly magnet, and grows well in all parts of California. But not all types grow equally well from the cool coast to inland areas, and most need pruning from time to time. But still it's an unforgettable butterfly experience.

FLOWER: Long, arching spires tightly crusted with lilac purple, yellow, orange, or bluish flowers over a long season.

PLANT: Upright or slightly cascading, gangly shrub, with thin foliage often silvery underneath.

INTERESTING KINDS: Summer lilac (*B. davidii*) is fast growing with fragrant flowers, and can re-grow if cut or frozen to the ground. Perhaps the most durable of all is the compact (needs less pruning) hybrid 'Lochinch', with gray foliage and light lavender blossoms well into late summer and fall.

California Coffeeberry
Rhamnus californica

Sun or part shade

This super drought-tolerant member of the "buckthorn" family is native to California and is used mostly as a background plant or hedge. Its berries are prized by birds.

FLOWER: Small clusters are barely noticeable, but berries turn from green to red to black as they ripen.

PLANT: Excellent hedge plant with narrow leaves that can be shiny or dull, green or yellowish, and usually lighter on the undersides.

INTERESTING KINDS: Several named selections that are generally shinier and greener than the wild species include 'Eve Case', 'Mound San Bruno', and a groundcover named 'Seaview'. Italian buckthorn (*R. alaternus*) is not as durable but is faster growing and gets up to 20 feet tall and wide. Redberry (*R. crocea*) is stiffer with spiny leaves and red berries.

California Lilac
Ceanothus species
Sun

Talk about native plants, this is a *biggee*. Though most are fairly short-lived when grown under typical garden conditions (too much irrigation), there is a huge, ever-changing variety on the market, all offering a great shot at using a true low-water-use native in the landscape.

FLOWER: Clusters, sometimes in spikes, of powder blue to cobalt to almost violet dark blue. Some are fragrant.

PLANT: Mostly evergreen, they range from bushy and compact to tall and airy, or spreading groundcover shrubs. Control size and spread by tip-pruning new growth after flowering. Must have good soil drainage!

INTERESTING KINDS: Too many to mention, but look for 'Blue Jeans', 'Concha', 'Dark Star', 'Frosty Blue', 'Julia Phelps', fall-blooming 'A.T. Johnson', 'Autumnal Blue' (blooms spring through autumn), C. × *pallidus* 'Marie Simon', and C. *thyrsiflorus* 'Blue Blossom' and 'Skylark' (summer bloomer).

Camellia
Camellia japonica
Light to moderate shade

Though these fall and mid-winter bloomers are prolific, and very low-maintenance once established, they grow best in a well-drained, somewhat acidic soil. Not many plants offer so much interest in mid-winter.

FLOWER: Double, semi-double, or single flowers in solids or variations of red, white, and pink, from late fall through mid-spring.

PLANT: Upright evergreen shrub with glossy green leaves up to 4 inches long. Loves plenty of mulch, requires good drainage to prevent root rot.

INTERESTING KINDS: Old standard C. *japonica* includes 'Pink Perfection', 'Tiffany', 'Debutante', 'Betty Sheffield', and 'Nuccio's Pearl' (or other Nuccio's). Smaller-flowered, fall-blooming types include C. *hiemalis* 'Shishi-Gashira' and C. *sasanqua* 'Apple Blossom', 'Yuletide', and 'Cleopatra'. There are many others.

Century Plant

Agave americana

Sun or part shade

This large, fierce-looking succulent makes a bold statement everywhere it is used (or overused), and is the hardest to get rid of once established. Bold accent for extreme dry conditions such as non-irrigated slopes, Western or desert themed gardens, or situated to keep trespassers from cutting through your property.

FLOWER: Mature plants produce tall pole-like stalks topped with short stems of yellow-green flowers, after which the "mother" plant dies, to be replaced with new "pups."

PLANT: Huge clump of thick, gray- or blue-green strap-shaped leaves, each edged with hooked spines and ending in a very sharp point.

INTERESTING KINDS: Several varieties have white- or yellow-striped leaves, including 'Marginata', 'Mediopicta', and 'Variegata'.

Coast Rosemary

Westringia fruticosa

Sun

This loose, spreading shrub from Australia looks and grows like rosemary (it is sometimes sold as *W. rosmariniformis*), and grows well close to the coast and in windy areas.

FLOWER: Small white flowers are produced nearly all year in warmer areas of the state, and from mid-winter through late spring in cooler areas.

PLANT: Wind-tolerant small shrub, usually up to 3 or so feet tall and wide. Grows best in light, well-drained soils like rosemary does.

INTERESTING KINDS: 'Wynyabbie Gem' has pale lavender flowers; *W. rigida* 'Morning Light' (variegated Australian rosemary) is smaller and more compact, with white-edged leaves; 'Smokey' has grayer leaves and a pale lavender tinge to the flowers.

Dragon Tree
Dracaena draco
Sun or part shade

Talk about other-worldly—this gangly Canary Island native is the largest hardy dracaena, and a perfectly acceptable, if bizarre, palm substitute.

FLOWER: Greenish white flowers form in small clusters on ends of branches, then drop off leaving small stems which can be clipped off (if you can reach them).

PLANT: Sturdy palm-like trunks branch out into stout limbs, each topped with a topknot of sword-shaped leaves. Tolerant of wind. Use similar to palms—a single plant for strong accent, or a small colony to create a tropical desert or jungle effect. Night lighting, either spotlight or backlight, creates spooky drama.

Escallonia
Escallonia species and cultivars
Sun or part shade

This clean-looking South American native is widely used for hedges and espaliers (trained against a wall or fence), with flowers as an added attraction.

FLOWER: Prolific pink, white, rosy red, or crimson flowers in small but showy clusters are produced in summer and fall (nearly all year in warm areas).

PLANT: Shiny leaves on upright or spreading plants that can be made fuller with occasional pinching or tip-pruning of new growth in the spring and summer.

INTERESTING KINDS: Many species and hybrids are on the market but the best known is *E. × exoniensis* 'Frades'; another is the hybrid 'Apple Blossom'; *E. rubra* is a popular hedge variety; 'Red Elf' is a dense, spreading variety; other species have compact forms.

Fatsia

Fatsia japonica

Part shade or full shade

Bold and tropical looking, this large evergreen shrub grows into a large mass in shaded areas, and works very well as an evergreen in large containers near a shaded pool or patio.

FLOWER: Round clusters of creamy white flowers produced above the foliage in the fall; small black berries may form in frost-free areas.

PLANT: Large, glossy, fan-like leaves over a foot wide on stems up to 6 feet tall. Shrubs spread by suckers. Leaves burn in sun. Tolerates a wide range of all but the wettest soils.

INTERESTING KINDS: Leaves of 'Variegata' have a creamy white or pale yellow edge; 'Moseri' is worth seeking out for its compact growth.

Firethorn

Pyracantha coccinea

Sun

A most spectacular apple relative with small late summer fruits that are actually edible, if bland.

FLOWER: Dense, flat clusters of small, dusty-fragrant blooms in the spring, followed by showy clusters of berries that turn from bright orange to red-orange by midsummer and persist until spring, when birds usually eat them.

PLANT: Upright evergreen shrub with small, oval leaves on sprawling limbs. Can be espaliered into interesting forms by pegging or tying to a wall. Branches have sharp thorns that cause painful punctures to the unwary.

INTERESTING KINDS: 'Lalandei' is very hardy; 'Gnome' is dense and only 6 or so feet tall. Other pyracanthas include hybrids with red berries ('Santa Cruz') and many compact varieties such as 'Lowboy' and 'Ruby Mound'.

Flowering Quince
Chaenomeles species
Sun or shade

An indestructible shrub, tolerant of every extreme of soil, that flowers in mid-winter, good for cutting.

FLOWER: Flattened, apple blossom-like flowers up to 2 inches across in scarlet, pink, white, orange, or salmon, produced on bare winter stems. May not bloom as prolifically in mild winters. Lemon-size, apple-like fruits.

PLANT: Long-lived with many thin branches, sparsely thorned; some forms have twisted, curly stems. Oval, serrated leaves are up to 3 inches long.

INTERESTING KINDS: *Chaenomeles speciosa* 'Apple Blossom' (white and pink); 'Contorta' (pinkish white with twisted branches, good for bonsai); 'Snow' (white); 'Coral Sea' (coral pink); 'Minerva' (cherry red); 'Red Ruffles' (ruffled red); and 'Toyo Nishiki' (tall, with pink, white, pink-and-white, and red flowers all on each stem, good fruits).

Hardy Dracaena
Cordyline australis
Sun

One of the best (and hardiest) palm substitutes—or better yet, where Joshua tree (*Yucca brevifolia*) is impractical such as near the seashore. Not a true dracaena but similar to the much coarser dragon tree (*Dracaena draco*).

FLOWER: Branches of fragrant but not showy flowers appear in the spring.

PLANT: Trunk-forming plant with a fat taproot is topped with a fountain of narrow, 3-foot leaves that droop as they get older. Grow near the seashore for a tropical look, or plant with large rocks and gravel mulch for a desert effect.

INTERESTING KINDS: Numerous cultivars, including bronze 'Atropurpurea'; 'Sundance', green with pink midrib; and 'Pink Stripe', bronze with pink margins.

Holly

Ilex species
Sun or light shade

Many species and cultivars of holly are used for hedges, specimens, and foundation plantings. Most are durable and need little or no pruning.

FLOWER: Insignificant wads of flowers clustered close to twigs in mid-spring; male and female plants must be planted close together for female berry production. Showy winter berries.

PLANT: Dense, mostly evergreen shrubs with shiny leaves, some with spines.

INTERESTING KINDS: Chinese holly (*I. cornuta*) is super tough, and includes compact 'Carissa', shrubby 'Dwarf Burford', and 'Rotunda'; *I. × altaclarensis* 'Wilsonii' has bright red berries and is well adapted to a wide range of soils; 'San Jose Hybrid' resembles 'Wilsonii' but is more upright and bears much heavier berries. Yaupon holly (*I. vomitoria*) is overlooked as a gray-green boxwood substitute that prunes well into tight balls; it has tree-form, weeping, and round compact varieties.

Honey Bush

Melianthus major
Part sun or light shade

A colony of honey bush is striking for its multiple stalks of saw-toothed gray leaves and bronzy-red flowers.

FLOWER: Striking foot-long flower spikes rise above the foliage with interesting rusty- or brick-red flowers that are nectar rich for birds.

PLANT: Moderately large suckering (spreading by runners) shrub with big, deeply divided, ruffled-edged leaves of distinctive gray or blue-green. When bruised, leaves release an unpleasant odor that reminds me of rancid peanut butter (its South African common name means "herb-touch-me-not"). Use as a backdrop for smaller shrubs, perennials, and grasses, where its legginess can be hidden. Children enjoy the fragrance, but its leaves are poisonous if eaten.

Hop Bush
Dodonaea viscosa
Sun or light shade

Native to the Southwest, Florida, and Hawaii, this short-lived but very tough shrub tolerates poor, dry soil, dry desert heat, and coastal wind, and works well as a hedge or specimen even in hot parking lot conditions.

FLOWER: Unnoticeable yellowish spring blooms lead to clusters of very showy, inch-long, yellow, pink, or red papery seedpods that last a long time (used in Hawaiian leis).

PLANT: Fast-growing with lots of upright stems covered with 4-inch willow-like leaves. Shrubs can get over 10 feet high and nearly as wide.

INTERESTING KINDS: 'Saratoga' has deep purple foliage; 'Purpurea' foliage starts out bronze and turns purple by winter. Note: Purple-leaf kinds need full sun or they fade to green.

Hydrangea
Hydrangea species
Sun or part shade

This old-fashioned shrub has large, almost tropical leaves and many large, stunning flowers.

FLOWER: Large round or oblong clusters of flowers that seem to last for months because parts are really sepals that maintain their color when dried. Very showy in spring and summer. Flowers are produced on new growth; severe winter pruning can limit flowers the following season.

PLANT: Rounded deciduous shrubs with large leaves. Need well-drained soil and lots of mulch in the summer.

INTERESTING KINDS: French or bigleaf or garden hydrangea (*H. macrophylla*) has large flowers in white, pink, rose, or blue (sometimes affected by acidity of the soil). Oakleaf hydrangea (*H. quercifolia*) is very showy, with deeply lobed leaves and football-size or larger clusters of white summer blooms.

Indian Hawthorn

Rhaphiolepis × delacourii

Sun or light shade

A virtually indestructible shrub for hot, sunny, dry spots, including parking areas and near beaches.

FLOWER: Dense spikes of pale pink, reddish, or white in spring and early summer, followed by dark blue fruits. Clipped shrubs rebloom constantly into fall.

PLANT: Evergreen shrub with glossy, leathery leaves that start out tinged with bronze or red. Can be trained into a small tree-form or pinched to keep it bushy. Leafspot diseases can be serious with over-irrigation, but heavy pruning after flowering removes much of the disease and stimulates new growth.

INTERESTING KINDS: 'Ballerina' is only 2 or 3 feet tall but wider; 'Enchantress' is huge—more like a small tree than a shrub; leafspot resistant strains include 'Indian Princess', 'Snow White', 'Olivia', and 'Snow Pink'. 'Majestic Beauty' is a wonderful small tree.

Italian Cypress

Cupressus sempervirens

Sun

This classic Mediterranean shrub is perhaps the most overused exclamation-point shrub in the state, but only looks bad when a row is planted, and the third one from the end dies.

FLOWER: No significant, but produces golf-ball size cones.

PLANT: Tall, narrow, tight evergreen spike with tiny scale-like leaves in green, blue-green, or tinged with golden yellow, depending on the cultivar. Note: Italian cypress often gets infested with leaf pests and diseases, but can be replaced with similar shrubs such as tecate cypress (*C. forbesii*), 'Skyrocket' juniper, or incense cedar (*Calocedrus decurrens*), and others. Use as a strong vertical accent, in tight spaces, as property line enhancement, or just to put on airs to neighbors.

Jerusalem Sage
Phlomis fruticosa
Sun

Exotic shrubs bring zest to California gardens and this Mediterranean native is one of the showiest.

FLOWER: Clusters (whorls) of oddly hooded yellow, purple, or lilac flowers are produced at leaf joints along entire stems in summer and fall. The stiff stems and long-lasting flowers are excellent as cut flowers or in dried arrangements.

PLANT: Upright stems with pairs of thick, oval, or lance-shaped furry leaves. Needs occasional watering in hot summer areas.

INTERESTING KINDS: Hybrid shrub-form 'Edward Bowles' has large, pure yellow flowers, and the compact plant resists oak root rot; *P. purpurea* has gray-green, narrow, lance-shaped leaves on white, wooly stems and purplish pink flowers mostly in the late spring. There are groundcover phlomis as well.

Junipers
Juniperus species
Sun or very light shade

In spite of their tendency to burn hotly in wildfires, junipers are versatile and important for their wide variety of shapes and landscape uses. Some quickly out-grow their sites.

FLOWER: Insignificant, but some species have light blue "berries" (used for flavoring gin).

PLANT: Evergreen mounds, spires, or spreading shrubs with tiny needle-like leaves of green, blue-green, silvery blue, purplish, golden, and variegated. Some are stiff and prickly, some soft. Junipers require well-drained soil, and cannot tolerate hard pruning.

INTERESTING KINDS: Pfitzer juniper (*J.* × *pfitzeriana*), at 6 feet and spreading, is often misplaced in too-small spaces; Gold Coast juniper (*J.* × *pfitzeriana* 'Gold Coast') is 3 feet by 5 feet with lacy, yellow foliage; blue point juniper (*J. chinensis* 'Blue Point') is a narrow, upright specimen to about 8 feet tall. Hollywood juniper (*J. chinensis* 'Kaizuka') can reach 20 feet and has a unique shape that makes it a good specimen plant.

Lemonade Berry
Rhus integrifolia
Sun

Interesting native plants are more popular and more commercially available than ever, and this one grows well in any soil. Plus it has fall color and you can make lemonade from the red summer fruits.

FLOWER: Showy clusters of small pinkish-white flowers are produced from late winter into summer, followed by small reddish berry-like fruits used to make a tart drink.

PLANT: Multiple-stem shrub that spreads by suckers over very poor ground. Oval leaves are dark green and leathery. Can be espaliered on fences or walls, or trimmed into a hedge as little as 1 foot wide.

INTERESTING KINDS: For small areas or slopes, or a large container, look for *Rhus typhina* 'Laciniata' with deeply dissected, fern-like leaves and showy red late summer and fall fruit.

Ligustrum
Ligustrum species
Sun or shade

Want an evergreen screen or small specimen tree fast and cheap? Ligustrum is your plant.

FLOWER: Showy, intensely fragrant white flower clusters are produced in mid-spring on un-pruned shrubs; late-summer black fruits are highly attractive to birds.

PLANT: Upright, spreading, evergreen shrub or small tree with oval leaves from 1 to over 3 inches long. Commonly sheared into tight specimens or hedges.

INTERESTING KINDS: Texas or waxleaf privet (*Ligustrum japonicum* 'Texanum') is possibly the most popular fast shrub for hedges; 'Rotundifolium' is a small shrub with twisted, curly leaves. Golden ligustrum ('Vicaryi') has golden foliage in full sun. Glossy privet (*L. lucidum*) is a dense evergreen tree getting over 30 feet high, but can be invasive if seedlings are not kept pulled from flower beds.

Manzanita
Arctostaphylos species
Sun or light shade

A classic California native with informal form and attractive limbs, perfect for underplanting with contrasting groundcovers for extreme low maintenance.

FLOWER: Clusters of small, urn-shaped flowers in white or pink in late winter or spring followed by red berrylike fruits which birds love.

PLANT: Evergreens with very attractive crooked branches with smooth, reddish bark. Loves poor soil and can survive on two or three soakings a summer (some tolerate irrigation but require good drainage). Plants don't tolerate heavy pruning; tip-prune new growth, or remove wayward branches entirely at their point of origin.

INTERESTING KINDS: 'Austin Hill' is smaller than the popular tall 'Dr. Hurd' and tolerates irrigation; 'Harmony' and 'Howard McMinn' are similar and widely available; 'John Dourley' has gray-green leaves, 3 feet tall and spreading. There are many others.

Myrtle
Myrtus communis
Sun or light shade

A Mediterranean garden would not be complete without this small aromatic shrub, whether used as an informal specimen or pruned into a tight little hedge plant or small topiary.

FLOWER: Small white flowers, about 3/4 inch across, with many frilly stamen, appear in summer along leafy stems, and are followed by 1/2-inch blue-black berries.

PLANT: Rounded small evergreen shrub with dense, fine-textured glossy green foliage with a pleasantly fragrant air when brushed. It withstands shearing very well, or can be limbed up as a small tree-form specimen

INTERESTING KINDS: 'Variegata' has white-edged leaves; 'Boetica' has unusual twisted trunks and limbs and large dark leaves; 'Compacta' is a dwarf form with small leaves, popular for low clipped hedges and Mediterranean rock gardens; 'Compacta Variegata' has white-margined leaves.

Nandina
Nandina domestica
Sun or shade

Heavenly bamboo—like it or not, it remains a carefree workhorse with year-round texture in the worst situations.

FLOWER: Billowy clusters of small white spring flowers are followed by showy clusters of pea-sized red fruits.

PLANT: Slow-spreading clump of slender stalks topped with stiff, ferny foliage that turns red in winter. Prune by thinning a few older canes nearly to the ground.

INTERESTING KINDS: Two fruitless kinds are 'Fire Power', a gnarly, twisted, red-and-burnt-orange compact form well suited for hot dry spots or mass planting; and 'Gulf Stream', a dense, dark-green mound with good red foliage in the winter. 'Harbor Dwarf' looks like "regular" nandina, but gets only 2 to 3 feet tall and spreads well; 'Compacta' gets to 5 feet tall and has good berry production.

New Zealand Flax
Phormium tenax
Sun or part shade

Rugged but freeze-sensitive, this large, fast-growing eruption of sword-like leaves gives instant drama, in groups or all by itself.

FLOWER: Tall spires of reddish-orange flowers with twisted seedpods.

PLANT: Short stems or stemless. Lots of long, narrow, pointed leaves held mostly upright. Use in large containers, on banks, in flower or shrub borders, beside swimming pools, anywhere strong lines are needed.

INTERESTING KINDS: Many colorful selections range from scarlet to bronze, chocolate brown to lime green, often with contrasting stripes (sometimes in pink or yellow) or different colors on upper and lower leaf surfaces.

Oleander

Nerium oleander

Sun

Perhaps the toughest shrub in California, this Mediterranean native grows equally well in coastal, mountain, and desert conditions—often seen in Interstate medians.

FLOWER: Single or double flowers, 2 or 3 inches wide, are in showy clusters from spring to fall, in white, red, pink, rose, salmon, and yellow, sometimes fragrant. Flowers of double-flowering forms can turn brown and persist.

PLANT: Upright limbs and many narrow leaves create a dense effect unless pruned into a small tree. Extremely hardy, though a serious disease transmitted by insects is getting worrisome in some areas. All parts of the plant are very poisonous if eaten.

INTERESTING KINDS: Compact forms include super-hardy 'Little Red', members of the Petite Series, 'Algiers', 'Casablanca', and 'Hawaii' (which drops its old flowers cleanly).

Oregon Grape Holly

Mahonia aquifolium

Sun or shade

This 4-season plant has everything: interesting form and foliage, late winter flowers, edible summer berries, and great fall and winter color. This shade-loving native plant can be pruned into an "architectural" specimen shrub, or allowed to spread into a mass.

FLOWER: Very showy chains of yellow bells appear at stem tips in late winter or early spring, followed by edible, blue, grape-like fruits.

PLANT: Spreading colony of upright stems with interesting whorls of shiny leaves, each up to a foot long with numerous spiny, holly-like leaflets. Leaves start out bronze, then deep green, and can turn reddish bronze in winter sun.

INTERESTING KINDS: 'Compacta' gets just over 3 feet high and spreads over twice that wide; 'Orange Flame' is smaller, with wine-red winter foliage.

Palms

Few plants say "exotic" better than palms, with their tall, swaying trunks and feathery or fan-shaped leaves, and interesting flowers and fruits. But they are flamboyant to the point of being easily overdone, making them one of the best landscape clichés around. Still, there are several great palms that grow well in most parts of California—enough choices for you to pick one that works, single stem or clump-forming, tall or squat.

Palms don't have "real roots" so they are easy to move or plant nearly any time of the year. Other than occasional deep soakings and light feedings, and plenty of mulch (partly to keep deadly string trimmers and mowers away from tender trunks), palms need only occasional grooming to remove badly tattered old leaf fronds. Here are a few selected hardy palms, but spend a little time with a local palm specialist before deciding which of these magnificent beauties you will be stuck with for many years to come!

Chinese Fan Palm (*Livistona chinensis*) is a tall palm with shiny green leaves up to 6 feetacross which droop downward at the edges. They even make great potted specimens. Australian fountain palm (*L. australis*) has dark green leaves and interesting leaf scars on its slender trunk.

Chinese Fan Palm

Palms to Avoid

Date palm (*Phoenix dactylifera*) does best in the hot Valley, and, like the *Washingtonia* palms, is generally too large for most home gardens anyway. The Canary Island date palm (*Phoenix canariensis*) is a severely invasive weed that spreads quickly from seed and is nearly impossible to dig up.

Jelly or Pindo Palm (*Butia capitata*) is named for its showy, edible, yellow or red summer fruits, jelly palm is a slow-growing species with a fat trunk and a tall arching crown of feathery gray-green leaves that spread over 10 feet wide. Most gardeners saw off the long-lasting leaf stubs to keep the plants more attractive.

Jelly or Pindo Palm

Lady Palm (*Rhapis excelsa*) in mature clumps look like stands of leafy bamboo. Slender trunks covered with dark sheaths are topped with deep green leaves. This is one of the most shade-tolerant palms and can be kept as a potted plant indoors for many years, or placed outside in a shaded location.

Mediterranean Fan Palm (*Chamaerops humilis*) is native to the Mediterranean region and is one of the hardiest palms and spreads slowly from offshoots into a clump up to 20 feet high and wide. Its fan-shaped leaves have spiny stalks. It can tolerate strong wind and very poor soils, even when massed under trees or when grown as a thick hedge.

Mediterranean Fan Palm

Mexican Blue Palm (*Brahea armata*) is one of the fan palms from Mexico, which also includes Guadalupe palm (*B. edulis*). It can take seaside conditions, wind, freezing weather, and hot deserts. Leaves of the blue palm are silvery blue, appearing almost white. Its long hanging flower stalks are loaded with very showy creamy white flowers.

Needle Palm (*Rhapidophyllum hystrix*) is native to the Southeastern U.S., this shrubby palm grows only to 6 or 8 feet tall. Its smooth stems grow from a very short trunk, with large, shiny, dark green leaves that are deeply cut (with a sharp tip on each leaflet, hence the name). Though hard to find ommercially except over the Internet, it is a sturdy palm for a wide variety of soils and conditions.

Needle Palm

Windmill Palm (*Trachycarpus fortunei*) is very hardy and is a fairly fast grower to over 20 feet tall. The trunk gets larger towards the top of the plant, with wooly fibers covering the upper section. Leaves up to 3 feet wide are on toothed stalks, and may become shredded in high winds. Young plants can easily be grown in pots, even in bright areas indoors; they can be set outside when they get too big for the house.

Windmill Palm

Pink Honey Myrtle
Melaleuca nesophila
Sun or part shade

Called honey myrtle because of its nectar-rich flowers, this bottlebrush relative is covered with nearly golf ball-size pinkish flowers for over half the year, from spring into fall.

FLOWER: Extremely profuse production of inch-wide, round flowers that are hummingbird and butterfly magnets.

PLANT: Medium to large shrub with gnarly branches of inch-long gray-green leaves. Grows well in both well-drained moist sites or rocky soils. Tolerates wet conditions, ocean spray, or desert heat.

INTERESTING KINDS: There are many species of *Melaleuca*, though most are hard to find commercially. M. *thymifolia* 'Pink Lace' and 'White Lace' have frilly, airy flowers. White bottlebrush tree or paperbark (M. *quinquenervia*) can become invasive in moist areas.

Pittosporum
Pittosporum tobira
Sun or part shade

Grown mostly for their generic shape and clean foliage, these common shrubs make good hedges, screens, windbreaks, and can be pruned as specimens to show off the irregular limbs. Dwarf forms are easy to keep clipped as foundation plants.

FLOWER: Creamy white or yellowish spring flowers smell like orange blossoms, and are sometimes followed by small orange fruit.

PLANT: Large, sturdy, rounded shrubs with shiny, dark-green, thumb-shaped leaves in tight whorls at the ends of twigs. Very tolerant of coastal wind conditions. Can be limbed up into a small tree.

INTERESTING KINDS: 'Variegatum' has grayish leaves with irregular, nearly-white margins. 'Wheeler's Dwarf' and 'Wheeler's Dwarf Variegata' are compact and only 3 to 4 feet high; 'Cream de Mint' is smaller with brighter green foliage edged in white.

Pomegranate
Punica granatum
Sun, part sun, part shade

Perhaps the most exotic Mediterranean fruit—called "fruit of the gods"—is produced on large shrubs with showy summer flowers. Some varieties have nice flowers but no fruit.

FLOWER: Large ruffled single or double orange-red flowers in spring and summer followed by large round leathery fruits packed with seeds encased in tart, juicy pulp.

PLANT: Dwarf to medium-size or large deciduous shrub with many stems (can be tip-pruned to keep it in bounds). Leaves are pointed ovals.

INTERESTING KINDS: Best fruiting varieties include 'Wonderful', 'Sweet', 'Eversweet', and 'Granada'. Flower-only varieties include 'Legrellei' ('California Sunset') with white flowers striped with red, dwarf *P. granatum* var. *nana* (may produce fruit), and 'Nochi Shibari' with double dark red flowers.

Red Tip Photinia
Photinia × fraseri
Sun or part shade

This occasionally overplanted large shrub is a popular and showy "red hedge" plant. It is very dependable except when planted too closely to one another in hedges, which crowds them and creates conditions for leaf diseases.

FLOWER: Showy flat clusters of white flowers in the spring followed by orange-red berries.

PLANT: Upright, dense shrub to 15 feet tall; can be kept sheared smaller. New growth is bright red, very attractive against older green leaves. Defoliating leafspot diseases are serious where shrubs are planted too close together (less than 6 feet apart) or irrigated too often.

INTERESTING KINDS: 'Birmingham' is the usual selection sold; 'Red Robin' is compact and has disease resistance.

Red Yucca

Hesperaloe parviflora

Sun

Too small to be considered oddball, this heat-tolerant New Mexico native resembles a thin-leaf yucca but is much tidier and can be more easily worked into dry flower borders, natural designs, or western- themed gardens. Also grows very well in highway medians or hot-area containers with little watering.

FLOWER: From late spring through fall, thin, branching, arching stems to 5 feet tall are produced, each covered for many weeks with flaring, tubular flowers of bright pinkish-red or red. Dried seed capsules the size of ping-pong balls are fairly attractive as well.

PLANT: Loose clumps of very thin evergreen leaves that are edged with fine, thread-like fringe tatters. Extremely low maintenance once established.

INTERESTING KINDS: 'Yellow' is a yellow-flowering form.

SOME PLANTS ARE "SHOW OFFS" IN THE LANDSCAPE. Just like bold statuary, these unique plants create a strong visual pull, leading the eye into or around large landscapes, and lend emotion and mood to smaller gardens. They are often used as focal points to draw attention toward good views, or to divert attention away from nearby bad views. As with anything good, each of these specimens can be overdone. Generally one per neighborhood is enough. Or in some cases, more than enough.

- Blue Puya
- Century Plant
- Dragon Tree
- Hardy Dracaena
- Hollywood Juniper
- Honey Bush
- Italian Cypress
- New Zealand Flax
- Ponytail Palm
- Prickly Pear Cactus
- Red Yucca
- Sago Palm
- Yucca

Rosemary

Rosmarinus officinalis

Sun

Classic Mediterranean native used as an accent, low hedge or barrier, and in containers—anywhere that is well drained. Hardy from seashore to inland parking-lot dividers.

FLOWER: Edible blue or white small flowers in clusters on stems bloom winter and spring, and occasionally in the fall. Good butterfly and bee attractant.

PLANT: Upright, mounded, or cascading evergreen with thin, almost conifer-like green leaves with gray undersides, very oily and aromatic and used widely as a food seasoning. Requires good drainage and benefits from occasional thinning to keep it vigorous.

INTERESTING KINDS: There is much variation between seedlings, so go with a named variety when possible (or root a piece from one you like). 'Blue Spires' and 'Tuscan Blue' make tall hedge plants.

Rose of Sharon or Althea

Hibiscus syriacus

Sun or light shade

This popular heirloom grows well everywhere except right along the coast in the Fog Belt and makes a sturdy long-lived specimen or hedge anywhere you plant it. Often flowers best a little inland in areas with hot/dry summers and cool winters.

FLOWER: Single or double hibiscus flowers in red, white, blue, pink, rose, and purple, often with contrasting eye color. Fruit capsules are attractive in the winter, but some single-flowering kinds self-seed everywhere.

PLANT: Upright vase-shaped deciduous shrub with many long, narrow branches and yellow fall color. Pruning is not needed, but you can thin to take out the clutter and increase flower size.

INTERESTING KINDS: 'Blue Bird' is true blue with a deep red eye; 'Red Heart' is white with a red eye. New sterile hybrids 'Diana', 'Helene', and 'Aphrodite' bloom better and longer, without going to seed.

Roses

Rosa species and hybrids

Full sun or very light shade

There are many very attractive, nearly pest-free rose varieties and species that are easy to
grow, from old-fashioned kinds found in country gardens to hot new varieties being developed
by new-age breeders.

FLOWER: Buds borne in loose masses open into many petals of red, white, pink, yellow,
orange, burgundy, near blue, and nearly every combination; some mature flowers remain tight
while others flop open shamelessly. Many are heady with fragrant perfume. Though some old
varieties bloom only once in the spring, most new kinds continue to flower off and on from
spring to fall. Pruning stimulates increased new flowering shoot and bud formation, but many
bloom repeatedly with no pruning at all.

PLANT: Small compact bushes to tall leggy shrubs, most with thorny branches. Though
foliage of many hybrids is susceptible to diseases (black spot and powdery mildew) for
which even regular fungicide sprays have only moderate success, many great roses are fairly
disease-free.

INTERESTING KINDS: In general, the most popular five kinds of roses are hybrid
tea (upright with long stems and pointed buds, most susceptible to diseases); polyantha (small
to medium bushes with solid masses of small flowers); floribunda (larger bushes with masses of
larger flower clusters); old garden roses (shrubby and climbing roses that have been around
since before the 1860s); and species roses (not hybrids, have been around forever). There are
others, of course.

'Knock Out' Rose

Felder's Picks: A Dozen Roses That Won't Break Your Heart

- **'Ballerina'** (pink and white shrub)

- **'Bonica'** (pink shrub)

- **'Carefree Delight'** (sturdy pink shrub)

- **'Cécile Brünner'** (pink polyantha)

- **'Duchesse de Brabant'** (fragrant old garden shrub)

Butterfly Rose

'La Marne'

- **'Europeana'** (red floribunda)

- **'First Edition'** (pink floribunda)

- **'Iceberg'** (white floribunda)

- **'Knock Out'** (ever-blooming red)

- **'La Marne'** (pink compact polyantha)

- **'Louis Philippe'** (mauve shrub)

- **'Mister Lincoln'** (red hybrid tea)

- *R. chinensis* **'Mutabilis'** or **Butterfly Rose** (large mixed-color shrub)

- **'Simplicity'** (pink floribunda)

- **'The Fairy'** (light-pink small polyantha)

There are many others, of course, including the native *Rosa californica* shrub rose ('Elsie' is a more uniform shrub with bigger pink flowers). These are a good start.

Sago Palm

Cycas revoluta

Sun or light shade

Not a true palm, this prehistoric plant survived whatever killed the dinosaurs! Victorian gardeners and contemporary designers alike love its contrast and texture.

FLOWER: Female plants produce many orange-red seeds in the center.

PLANT: Mounded form comes from the rosettes of long, wide, feathery leaves that emerge in one or two flushes a year. New growth is soft and pale yellow-green, but quickly hardens into stiff, deep-forest-green fronds that persist for a year or more. Propagate by twisting small "pups" from the base and potting them up for a year or so until established. Use as an accent by a doorway, a primitive tropical effect in a collection of plants, or as a very long-lived container specimen.

INTERESTING KINDS: Cardboard palm (*Zamia furfuracea*) is a compact sago relative with very stiff, almost wood-like leaflets each up to 4 inches long and over an inch wide. Mostly grown as a potted specimen.

Shrubby Yew Pine

Podocarpus macrophyllus var. maki

Sun or part shade

Commonly grown heat-tolerant hedge, specimen, or container plant, very upright and narrow, that can be espaliered or made into a topiary.

FLOWER: Insignificant flowers, but if a male is planted nearby female plants may develop small, red, fleshy fruits.

PLANT: Dense evergreen shrub, upright to 15 or more feet tall but only 4 to 5 feet wide, with thin, dark green leaves 3 inches long and $^{1}/_{4}$ inch wide. Very easy to maintain as a narrow hedge or an accent.

INTERESTING KINDS: The "regular" yew pine (*Podocarpus nagi*), a 30- to 50-foot monster, has long been abused by being planted where gardeners expected it to stay small. *Podocarpus nagi* is another evergreen shrub for hedges or containers whose branches become pendulous or weeping as the plant ages.

Spirea
Spiraea species
Sun or moderate shade

Spireas are sturdy spring-blooming mainstays that double as backdrops for smaller summer flowers.

FLOWER: Clusters of small single or double white flowers along arching stems in the spring; the more shrubby spireas can be pink, white, or red, blooming late spring through summer.

PLANT: Durable, long-lived deciduous or semi-evergreen shrubs with small leaves.

INTERESTING KINDS: Baby's breath spirea (*S. thunbergii*) has clusters of small single flowers; bridal wreath (*S. prunifolia*) has button-like double flowers; Reeves spirea (*S. cantoniensis*) has flowers grouped around leaves in mid-pring ('Flore Pleno' is a double flowering form); and Van Houtte spirea (*S. × vanhouttei*) is the latest bloomer with 2-inch flat clusters. Summer-blooming, compact *S. japonica*, which grows very well in Valley gardens, includes pink 'Anthony Waterer', 'Gold Mound' (chartreuse foliage), and 'Limemound' (lime-green turning gold in the fall).

Viburnum
Viburnum species
Sun or part shade

There are many different viburnums, most overlooked by "garden variety" gardeners because they aren't very impressive at garden centers. But in the landscape they are versatile and have a wide variety of flowering habits.

FLOWER: Springtime white or pinkish flowers in clusters from 2 to 6 inches across, sometimes with an odd, dusty smell; many have showy fruit as well.

PLANT: Medium to large shrubs, evergreen or deciduous. Most have handsome foliage, some with fall color.

INTERESTING KINDS: *Viburnum tinus* 'Spring Bouquet' is super compact and floriferous; sandankwa viburnum (*V. suspensum*) has flower clusters up to 4 inches across. I love the various snowball viburnums with huge white flower heads in spring.

Yucca

Yucca species

Sun or very light shade

In spite of losing a childhood inflatable beach ball to a stiff yucca, there are plenty that are not as dangerous. Use as a vertical accent and interesting silhouette against buildings. Group with agaves and cactus, or as contrasting texture in shrub borders, and dormant season accent for perennial gardens.

FLOWER: Tall spikes of usually creamy white bell-shaped flowers, which are perfectly edible.

PLANT: Long, narrow, stiff leaves with pointed tips radiate from the center of the plant, with or without a stem or trunk. Some are very sharp and stiff, others have softer foliage that makes them look worse than they really are. Some gardeners snip the pointed tips off to reduce accidental contact.

INTERESTING KINDS: Many forms, from small groundcovers to large specimens, some with leaf edges or centers of yellow or cream.

Other Good Shrubs:

Australian Fuchsia (*Correa* species) is a tough fuchsia substitute, but won't tolerate a lot of heat.

Bush Poppy (*Dendromecon rigida*) is a native with showy yellow flowers, but gets leggy and needs pruning, especially along coastal areas

Cape Honeysuckle (*Tecoma capensis*) and **Yellow Bells** (*Tecoma stans*) are very beautiful but marginal in interior Valley areas.

Cleyera (*Ternstroemia gymnanthera*) is a good generic green shrub with fragrant if not showy flowers, but needs pruning to keep it in bounds, and turns yellow in alkaline (normal) soil.

Elaeagnus (*Elaeagnus pungens*) gets too big and wild-looking, period. Tough though.

Euonymus (*Euonymus japonicus*) is a very popular evergreen shrub for inland areas, usually with yellow or white variegation, and is easy to prune—which is good because scale insects and mildew on the leaves make it necessary to tidy the plant frequently.

Flowering Maple (*Abutilon* species) has wonderful bell-shaped flowers loaded with nectar for hummingbirds, but is pest prone and needs regular pruning.

Gardenia (*Gardenia augusta*) is very popular for its super-fragrant white flowers; everyone wants to grow it but most fail because it requires perfect soil and perfect irrigation, and then dies anyway.

Gold Jasmine (*Cestrum aurantiacum*) and other cestrums have beautiful tubular flowers that attract hummingbirds, but are not universally hardy and need pruning.

Golden Dewdrop (*Duranta erecta* 'Gold Mound') is a favorite of mine, but needs regular thinning and pruning to keep in bounds, and is not as tough in the Central Valley.

Grevillea (*Grevillea* species) includes lots of very good plants, including 'Red Hooks' with interesting foliage and flowers. But they have sensitive roots and are risky in "garden variety" gardens.

Lion's Tail (*Leonotis leonurus*) is a many-stemmed, upright shrub with dense whorls of rich orange tubular flowers in summer and fall. Looks best with regular pruning.

Pearl Acacia (*Acacia podalyriifolia*), while not as invasive as acacias on the invasive plant list, needs regular pruning to remain compact and won't tolerate irrigation.

Rockrose (*Cistus laurifolius*) is a carefree, drought-tolerant grayish shrub with showy 2- to 2$\frac{1}{2}$-inch-wide white, pink, purplish-pink, spring and summer flowers. It can grow from seashore to mountain to desert—without irrigation. And it is fire resistant.

Sagebrush (*Artemisia californica*) is similar to buckwheat in its low maintenance.

Wild Buckwheat (*Eriogonum* species) is a durable native that looks ragged without pruning and resents irrigation and fertilizer, making it unsuitable for mixing with "tame" plants.

Poodle Plants

Every neighborhood from upscale to working class has one. "Floating Clouds (Ukigumo, or "green balls on sticks") is the most common form of topiary, proving to neighbors that the owner pays great attention to detail and has pride in workmanship. Like a Mohawk haircut—you either strongly like or strongly dislike them.

Various evergreen plants can be used this way, but most often they're junipers. There are two basic forms: either irregular multiple stems ending in tightly sheared balls, or a single stem with balls stacked formally one atop another. Not low maintenance, but they can make interesting entry accents, formal container specimens, or oriental garden effects.

Help! I'm a Garden Nerd!

Ever find a sprig of rosemary soaking in a water glass beside the sink, left over from a nice meal out on the town the evening before? Anyone who brings food home to root has a problem, possibly an addiction.

There should be a 12-step Gardeners Anonymous program, for those who garden every day, spend family money on plants (often just because they are on sale, needed or not), and can't keep focused on anything else when driving around town.

Can't you just hear it now? "Hi, I'm Felder, and I am a gardener." ("Welcome, Felder, we are glad you are here. Come back often.")

Sound close to home? Here's a simple test to see if you, too, need help:

- Do you grow ten or more different kinds of the same plant (succulent, orchid, African violet, wildflower, whatever), and know their names? Extra points if they're labeled.
- Do you subscribe to three or more garden magazines?
- Do you keep a small shovel in your car trunk? Buy birdseed by the fifty pound sack? Own a $40 pair of pruning shears (bonus points for a leather holster)? Are entire flats of flowers still sitting in the driveway because there's simply no more space to plant?
- Have you ever willingly taken a tour of a garden by flashlight? Do we need to search your purse or camera case for purloined seeds after a visit to a botanical garden?
- Are your cuticles dirty right now? Do you know the name of your county Extension Service horticulturist? Do the loading guys at the local garden center know you by name?
- And last, but not least, triple points of you would appreciate a special someone sending you a load of manure for an anniversary...

I'm not suggesting we gardeners should quit—though we all claim we can, any time. Maybe our motto should be One Flower at a Time. And remember, denial is a symptom!

SAVVY
Succulents

Some succulents get through dry spells by storing water in their swollen stems or leaves. Some have very small leaves during wet seasons, which shed during dry spells. A few use spines to help keep predators away, while others just drop fat leaves everywhere, which quickly sprout into entire new plants. A good many of these desert-dwellers (both tropical and temperate) grow on sunlight and rainfall alone, others need occasional light feedings. Most will deflate and die if grown like jungle plants with lots of water.

Ball O'Succulents

The world of succulents is huge, with many avid collectors scattered all over California (many of whom will argue over the tiniest variation between the exact same plants). But they get together for regular plant sales, where you can find sometimes rare, always-easy jewels for your garden.

Many of the following plants can be grown outdoors in all parts of California; however, many are grown in containers just to control the amount of water they get (and to keep them away from suffocating fog), and to bring them in during a sudden deep freeze in interior counties. They all need bright, indirect light. There are many others, and countless variations between them all. This is just a teensy start.

 **Best for Beginners:**

- *Dwarf Opuntia*
- *Pencil Cactus*
- *Jade Plant*

Kinda Tricky: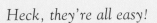

- *Kalanchoe*

  Heck, they're all easy!

Aeonium
Aeonium species

Exotic foliage on succulent stems, these are consistently among the most decorative, whether in bloom or not, especially in pots clustered near entryways or on steps where visitors can slow down and admire. Can be grown in the ground except in areas of hard freezes. Too many very interesting kinds to even begin listing, but one of the most stunning is 'Zwartkop' with nearly black leaves.

Bulbine
Bulbine frutescens

At first this seems like an interesting clump of nearly succulent, pointy, pencil-leaves, and its nearly non-stop spikes of bright yellow or orange flowers are showy. Then the plant continues to spread into a nearly impenetrable groundcover in dry, well-drained areas. Not for hot sunny spots or areas where foot traffic is likely to slip on its slickness.

Bunny Ears
Opuntia microdasys

Talk about bringing the countryside indoors—even though perfectly hardy outdoors in nearly the entire state, this and other miniature prickly pears make charming potted specimens in sunny spots indoors or out. All are easily rooted from "pads" simply pushed into potting soil.

Burn Plant
Aloe vera

Rosettes of narrow, upright leaves with short spines on the edges, very thick and succulent (sap has long been used medicinally to soothe cuts and burns). Leaves are up to a foot long. Flowers are yellow and produced on a dense spike up to 3 feet long. Frost tender. There are many different aloes, including the giant multi-trunk tree aloe (A. *arborescens*) that gets to 10 feet tall.

Carrion Cactus or Starfish Cactus
Stapelia species

This old pass-along plant spreads with many jointed, four-sided stems 6 to 9 inches long. When it flowers, the large, unusual pointed buds open into sprawling, five-pointed flat stars surrounding a circular fleshy disk. Depending on the species, flowers are yellowish or purplish with darker spots or bars. They smell like dead meat as a way to attract pollinating flies.

Crown of Thorns
Euphorbia milii var. *splendens*

Frost-sensitive shrub with slender, upright branches armed with many sharp spines and thin, roundish leaves. Fairly continuously topped with loose clustered pairs of small flowers in red, orange, yellow, or pink. The stems root readily. Its milky sap is characteristic of all euphorbias.

Devil's Backbone
Pedilanthus tithymaloides ssp. *smallii*

In the tropics, this densely stemmed tropical shrub is grown even in cemeteries. It can get to waist high or taller and 3 feet across in frost-free parts of California. Sometimes called "red bird cactus" because its red flowers resemble birds in silhouette, this milky-sap succulent has branched, crooked stems which zigzag at each leaf joint. Leaves can be plain green or green-and-white variegated, with a touch of pink in sunny gardens.

Donkey Tail or Burro Tail
Sedum morganianum

Popular hanging basket or cascading container plant with many long, hanging "tails" to 4 feet or more, densely matted with overlapping thick, gray-green fleshy leaves. Can have red flowers near bottom tips of branches but it's a rare occurrence. Very easy to root and start new plants. Protect from gusty winds or bring indoors and place near a sunny window.

Ghost Plant or Hens and Chicks
Graptopetalum paraguayense

Hardy down into the 20-degree range, this common potted plant (another of many sometimes called "hens and chicks") has tight roses of thick, clunky gray-green leaves on stems up to a foot or more long. When they break apart (as they always do), all parts will root, including leaves, which form little plants on the stem end.

Golden Barrel Cactus
Echinocactus grusonii

While hardy outdoors in much of the state, this stocky, slow-growing Mexican native is still a natural for growing in large, low pots as an accent—that can be moved around a lot easier than one growing in the ground! Prominent ribs and short, stout thorns give an interesting texture that no one wants to tangle with.

Haworthia or Fairy Washboard
Haworthia attenuata

Of all the many varied members of this South African tribe of succulents—which has several fan clubs and web pages—one of the most common grows in clumps of small, tight rosettes with short, pointed leaves heavily marked with raised white spots. It grows best in extremely porous potting mixes and thrives without rotting on little or no water. Flowers are occasionally produced on long arching stems.

Hens and Chicks
Echeveria species and *Sempervivum tectorum*

If you know how closely a mother hen keeps her chicks nestled underneath, you can figure out where these plants get their common name. Both kinds of plants are easy-to-share potted plants or rock garden additions that form dense mats of short, easy-to-root stems ending in tight rosettes. Flowers on some are showy.

Jade Plant
Crassula ovata

It is jokingly said that you should water this thick-trunked shrub with its fat, thumb-size leaves at least once every twenty-five years—not much of an exaggeration since it can go months with no water at all. This superb container specimen, which makes a dense, stout hedge plant in Southern California, is among the easiest tropical plants to grow, unless you over-water it. Flowers are clustered and star-shaped. There are variegated and red-tinged forms, including 'Tricolor' with green-white-and-pink foliage.

Kalanchoe
Kalanchoe blossfeldiana

This popular Mother's Day florist gift plant (correctly pronounced kah-len-CO-e) has very showy clusters of hot pink, red, yellow, or orange flowers, and can live for years in its original pot, on air and water alone. Pinching or rooting pieces can thicken it up, but getting it to rebloom is a little tricky—it is a "short day" plant, like poinsettia, so you have to fool it into thinking days are getting short to stimulate flower production.

Mother of Thousands or Maternity Plant
Kalanchoe daigremontiana

One of the most unusual plants commonly passed around between gardeners, this fleshy-leaf succulent has long, arrowhead shaped leaves that are spotted with purple, and many toothed notches along the edges in which small plantlets are produced—complete with leaves and roots of their own—which fall off and sprout nearly everywhere.

Night-Blooming Cereus
Hylocereus and *Selenicereus* species

This popular pass-along plant has several forms—some with long, almost vine-like three-ribbed leaves, others with long, flat, toothed leaves more like jagged swords—that climb and sprawl and attach to other plants or supports with strong aerial roots. Their large, exotic, white or pinkish flowers open only at night and are completely spent by the next morning, but plants can bloom all summer. Fruits are edible and sweet.

Pencil Cactus
Euphorbia tirucalli

This plant is sometimes called "milk bush" because of its thick shrubby growth and milky sap. This tall, twiggy oddity may be the most passed-around potted plant in the country. Not a cactus at all (it's in the same family as poinsettia), it is named for its thin, cylindrical, thornless stems, which look like lots of green pencils stacked end-to-end. Tiny green leaves appear occasionally. 'Sticks on Fire' has shocking reddish stems that fade to golden yellow in the summer sun.

Prickly Pear Cactus
Opuntia species

The absolute hardiest cactuses in the world, instantly recognized by their flat, round "Mickey Mouse ears" leaf pads. Strikingly beautiful yellow or orange daisy-like blooms with many small narrow petals, followed by egg-size berries filled with moist, delicious, blood-red juice and many small seeds. Peel before eating to avoid lips full of tiny stickers! There are many varieties, mostly upright or sprawling masses of flattened "leaves" (really modified green stems) that are round or oblong, large or small, very thorny or covered in small spines but occasionally smooth. Edible pads (*nopales*) can be grilled and sliced, or sliced and sautéed (*nopalitos*).

Rock Purslane
Calandrinia grandiflora

One of the "hot" succulents is a native of Chile that forms mounds over 2 feet tall with fleshy gray-green leaves up to half a foot long. The plant needs extremely well-drained soil and only occasional watering. What makes it really showy are the spring stalks of big, 2-inch-wide purple flowers.

Soap Aloe
Aloe saponaria

Along with the old familiar *Aloe vera* there are other dependable forms for colonizing dry areas or use in containers. Perhaps the hardiest is soap aloe, with foot-wide flattened rosettes of fleshy leaves spotted with white, topped with 2¹/₂ foot sprays of shrimp pink, red orange, or yellow flowers.

Stonecrop
Sedum species

Many species of this large family of succulent plants are hardy outdoors; some have trailing branches, others are upright shrubs, with highly variable leaf shapes, sizes, and colors. If the species names like *lineare*, *rubrotinctum*, *kamtschaticum*, *spathulifolium*, *spurium*, *stoloniferum*, and *confusum* scare you off, just look around and see which sedums catch your fancy and jump in. They're easy, as long as you don't water a lot.

The Plant-Society-a-Day Garden

Ever meet someone who thinks that one kind of plant is the best of all, with everything else in Eden being a mere "companion?" I'd rather like to have a few of every kind—to have a "plant society a day" represented in one garden.

Irises come in every color of the rainbow, but some are hard to grow in all of California. Same with daffodils, though you can try refrigerating bulbs and all that horticulture stuff. Primroses? Their society headquarter is in Juneau, Alaska. What's the point?

There are roses, of course, though most of us have been burned by fussy hybrid teas. I prefer "gardener friendly" heirlooms, including old timers such as 'Old Blush' and 'Cécile Brünner' (the old sweetheart rose), and not-so-antique 'Knockout' and 'The Fairy'. America's Floral Emblem isn't hard to grow if you choose easy varieties.

We all enjoy our daylilies; the long-blooming 'Stella d'Oro' miniature is almost a garden cliché. But my all-time favorite is the old double orange 'Kwanso', grown for eons all over the world. Though nearly impossible to find in a daylily society display, it grows for me, you, anybody, anywhere, with absolutely no demands. None.

There's the camellia, the "rose of winter," and herbs, including rosemary and mint, which I cook with and also grow as "just good plants." Most likely you have a palm and a hibiscus in your garden, and probably a bromeliad or two; there are societies for them all.

Let's see, that's seven plant societies represented in typical California gardens: rose, iris, camellia, daylily, herbs, palms, and hibiscus. Add wildflowers and your garden will be fit for a plant society a day.

Oh, and there's a support group for cacti, succulents, orchids, dahlias, African violets, and gourds, plus tropical fruits. There ought to be a Compost Club, and a Faded Poinsettia Society—there's gotta be millions of honorary members. How about a Friends of Half-Hardy Plants (motto: Good Luck!)...

Better yet, an all-encompassing Companion Plant Coalition!

STOUTHEARTED
Trees

Trees are the big items in your landscape. Because they are so dramatic in size and effect, trees provide the most important landscape framework for your garden, apart from your home and other structures. Trees enclose and shade the landscape, and provide nesting places and food for wildlife.

Redwoods

For average-size gardens, large trees can be disruptive. They take a long time to grow, have invasive roots that can lift sidewalks, are greedy for sunlight and water, and may require pruning and other maintenance. In most cases, small trees or very large shrubs are better choices. For this reason this chapter deals with only a few of the very toughest small trees planted in garden-type landscapes. Most make fine specimens or stand-out trees because of their flowers or foliage. Some are easy to work into existing beds, others make good shade for more tender plants, and several are excellent "understory" or "in between" plants.

It's an oddball fact, but a small tree will outgrow a larger tree of the same species if planted at the same time, nearly every time. Choosing a tree that is smaller can also be important both for your wallet and your back. Even if you plant small specimens, keep in mind that trees need elbowroom to grow. Meanwhile, nothing beats a clean layer of natural mulch to make trees "look right" while protecting the new roots from hot summer sun, cool nights, and attacks from lawn mowers and string trimmers. Plus, as leaves and bark decompose, they feed the soil around tree roots in a natural way.

Protect Your Trees

Just one deep gash on the tender bark of a young tree can interfere with food movement from leaves to roots, which causes the tree to suffer for years to come. Prevent this common cause of tree death by mulching around the base, edging with bricks, rocks, or another ornate shield, or a groundcover. Keep in mind that two or more trees can be "connected" at their bases by a large mulched area, in which small shade-loving shrubs or perennials can be planted.

Protect vital roots of mature trees from anything that will cut, compact, or bury them, and avoid over-watering and over-fertilizing, which can rot roots and force heavy top growth that the roots may not be able to support in strong gusty winds.

Getting Trees in the Ground

To encourage tree roots to get established quickly, and to roam far and wide, they need to grow roots out into the native soil quickly. There is no need to

CITRUS TREES ARE ALMOST IRRESISTIBLE, but are certainly not low maintenance. Most kinds require very well-drained soils kept uniformly moist, with faithfully regular feeding, and occasional pruning—not to mention all that harvesting and eating labor!

Most citrus trees grow best in warm or hot summers and mild winters, and even hardy kinds suffer during sudden frosts. 'Improved Meyer' lemon is perhaps the most dependable citrus "yard tree," though edible-skin kumquats are very durable and can withstand freezes. For more information on the best citrus for your area, contact your Extension Service home garden advisor.

Street Trees, Lawn Trees

Note that almost every city has a list of appropriate ("approved") trees for planting along streets. If you haven't run up against this, you will soon. Check first before planting between your sidewalk and curb. And while I'm at it—planting trees in lawns is a common design error with long term problems; they not only look weirdly out of place, but are water guzzlers and maintenance nightmares.

add too much "stuff" to your soil when planting trees, just enough to get them started. Here are a few quick planting tips for trees:

- Dig a *wide* hole, not a deep one, loosening the sides and bottom of the hole. If the soil is too hard to dig, mound it up and plant the tree in the raised area.
- Set the tree so its original soil line is even with or a little higher than the soil around it.
- Fill in around roots with original soil (with the soil from the tree's container mixed in).
- Make a ring of soil around the planting site to make watering easier the first year or so.
- Loosely stake new trees for a year or two to keep them from falling over in high wind while the rootball anchors itself in the new soil.
- Cover the planting area with leaves, bark, or other natural mulch.
- Water deeply, not frequently, to encourage roots to grow quickly both to the sides and down.

Lilac Chaste Tree at the Copia Center, Napa

Chinese Pistache
Pistacia chinensis
Sun

One of the best trees for fall color in mild-winter areas, even in the desert, this reliable street, lawn, or patio tree withstands extreme drought in deep soils, but also tolerates irrigation.

FLOWER: Barely noticeable, but if male and female trees are planted near one another, females may produce tiny, inedible fruits.

PLANT: Spreading tree with glossy green leaves that are divided into many leaflets that turn bright orange to red in the fall.

INTERESTING KINDS: Mount Atlas pistache (*P. atlantica*) is widely used as a rootstock for fruiting pistachio trees and makes a fine, very drought-tolerant tree on its own. Mastic (*P. lentiscus*) has red to black fruit, tolerates very hot, dry areas and produces an aromatic resin from its sap. Not widely available.

Chitalpa
× *Chitalpa tashkentensis*
Sun

This rugged hybrid between two natives—large-flowering catalpa (*Catalpa bignonioides*) and the tough desert willow (*Chilopsis linearis*)—has the best of both parents. The light shade it provides and its regular shedding of flowers make a pleasant tree to sit under.

FLOWER: Frilly inch-long trumpets of pink, white, or lavender, with a yellow landing strip for hummingbirds, appear all summer and into fall. Fragrance is light, and flowers shed neatly.

PLANT: Fast-growing small deciduous tree with narrow leaves up to 5 inches long, which may shed a few at a time during dry spells.

INTERESTING KINDS: 'Pink Dawn' has uniformly pink flowers; 'White Cloud' has white. The parent plants, large-leaf catalpa and desert willow (with more flower colors), grow poorly along the So-Cal coastline.

Coral Tree
Erythrina crista-galli
Sun

A most unusual specimen plant with strong structural form and brilliant red summer flowers. Requires no irrigation at all during dry spells.

FLOWER: Unusual flowers appear in two or three waves over the summer, bright red and followed by bean-like seedpods with orange-red seeds.

PLANT: Large shrub with many rough, slightly thorny stems that produce 6-inch leaves divided into three leaflets. Woody base is nearly impossible to dig, so plant this hulking beauty where it can stretch without needing to be moved. Evergreen in warm-winter areas and "woody herbaceous" in cooler areas.

INTERESTING KINDS: Several tender species are available as potted plants, including natal coral tree (*E. humeana*) with long stalks of narrow orange-red flowers.

Crape Myrtle
Lagerstroemia hybrids
Sun

The "summer lilac" is a four-season plant, with good form, impressive summer flowers, fall foliage color, and sensuous bare limbs in winter. Hybrids resist powdery mildew better than the species.

FLOWER: Large, football-shaped clusters of crinkly flowers in white, pink, red, lavender, and mixed. Not fragrant. Blooms are shed neatly as a colorful carpet on the ground underneath.

PLANT: Upright with either a single or multiple trunks, smooth to the point of feeling slick, tan with large patches of cinnamon red. Easy to prune into tree form, or keep bushy with regular pinching of new growth.

INTERESTING KINDS: Look for Native American tribal names such as 'Natchez', 'Biloxi', 'Sioux', 'Hopi', and the like. 'Dynamite' has red flowers, with reddish buds and new foliage. These hybrids are still susceptible to mildew along coastal areas, but are much less so than the common species crape myrtle (*L. indica*).

Fern Pine
Podocarpus gracilior
Sun or part shade

One of the most useful, pest-free, clean trees for planting near patios or driveways. Can also be grown as a large shrub, trimmed into a hedge plant, or planted in large pots.

FLOWER: Not significant, but if pollinated by a nearby male, female specimens may produce small, fleshy, berry-like fruit.

PLANT: Dark, glossy leaves are narrow and up to 4 inches long. Mature trees develop grayish or blue-green leaves. Rooted branches are very limber and grow better as vines tied to fences or even in hanging baskets.

INTERESTING KINDS: Yellowwood (*P. henkelii*) has masses of drooping, shiny green leaves and a narrow, upright form; this is a large evergreen shrub suitable for hedges or topiary. *Podocarpus latifolius* has stiffer, smaller leaves.

Fig
Ficus carica
Sun or part sun

The true Mediterranean fig tree is a traditional favorite of gardens that have the elbowroom for it to spread out. Sweet figs are a special treat, fresh or dried.

FLOWER: Roundish "fruits" are actually inverted flowers—look closely inside and see for yourself.

PLANT: Mounding tree to 30 feet tall and nearly as wide with several heavy trunks and smooth gray bark. Leaves are large, lobed, and sandpapery. Can be espaliered against a wall. Tolerant of many soils and drought.

INTERESTING KINDS: 'Brown Turkey' can make two crops per year; purple-skinned 'Mission' is very popular; 'Texas Everbearing' has purplish brown skin, reddish flesh, and produces well in a very short season for hot areas; and 'Violette de Bordeaux' ('Negronne') is good for container culture or small spaces.

Ginkgo
Ginkgo biloba
Sun

The prehistoric "maidenhair" tree, so-called because its leaves resemble maidenhair fern foliage, has good form and foliage, and interestingly shaped leaves that provide dependable fall color throughout the state.

FLOWER: Not significant, but female selections can develop a fleshy fruit that is messy and foul-smelling, especially noticeable when the mature trees are planted near pedestrian areas.

PLANT: Variable form but generally an upright tree with flat, fan-shaped, medium green leaves that turn bright yellow in the fall all at one time, hang for a few days, then shed uniformly into a carpet of gold.

INTERESTING KINDS: Seed-grown species are highly variable; choose named male cultivars with predictable form, including the broadly spreading 'Autumn Gold', pyramidal 'Fairmount', or narrow, tapering 'Princeton Sentry'.

Golden Rain Tree
Koelreuteria paniculata
Sun or light shade

This somewhat weedy tree, which can be controlled easily with regular pulling or cutting of seedlings, is a mainstay for low-maintenance landscapes. It thrives on little or no care, and has several seasons of interest.

FLOWER: Very showy foot-long clusters of yellow flowers turn to reddish fruit capsules that become papery as they mature to light brown; the dried pods are used in floral arrangements.

PLANT: Rounded tree to 40 feet tall and nearly as wide, with ferny compound leaves that start out purplish, turn bright green in the summer, and have yellow fall color.

INTERESTING KINDS: The species is a very dependable tree but 'Rose Lantern' has rose-pink seed capsules and 'Fastigiata' gets 25 feet tall but only 3 or 4 feet wide.

Japanese Persimmon
Diospyros kaki

Sun

This small shade tree loads up with large, ornamental, delicious fall fruit. It also has dependable fall color, even in mild climates.

FLOWER: Not noticeable, but more than makes up for it with orange or reddish fall fruit. Cross-pollinated varieties have the best taste, but self-fruitful kinds are seedless. Non-astringent kinds don't make you pucker up when eating. Fruit drop is common on young plants that are allowed to stay very dry.

PLANT: Rounded tree usually with a single trunk and almost gnarly branch patterns. Can be espaliered easily. Thick, oval leaves turn yellow, red, and orange in the fall.

INTERESTING KINDS: All are great. 'Fuyu' is like a slightly flattened orange baseball, self-fruitful, and non-astringent; 'Chocolate' is acorn-shaped with dark streaks in the flesh when pollinated; 'Izu' is a dwarfish new cultivar.

Jerusalem Thorn or Palo Verde
Parkinsonia aculeata

Sun

If you never want to water again, this Mexican native is your tree. Its airy "desert" look complements wildflowers and cactuses, and is dramatic against a building in a hot, dry site.

FLOWER: Showy yellow flowers in loose clusters on 6- to 7-inch stems that hang down, produced in spring and after rains in the summer; followed by long bean pods.

PLANT: Fast-growing but unpredictable form to 25 or more feet tall with yellow-green bark and sparse, zigzag thorny branches that are useful in dried flower arrangements. Leaves are sparse, with many tiny leaflets that shed in drought or cold weather.

INTERESTING KINDS: Only the species is available.

Lilac Chaste Tree
Vitex agnus-castus
Sun or very light shade

Vitex is an old-garden plant that is making a huge comeback as a specimen plant when limbed up near a patio or along a sidewalk, with spikes of summer flowers attractive to bees, butterflies, and hummingbirds.

FLOWER: Upright panicles to nearly a foot long crusted with small blue, lavender, pink, or white flowers, produced from late spring into midsummer or later.

PLANT: Small, rounded, umbrella-like tree, multi-trunked with grayish brown bark and many branches of dense, aromatic leaves used in ancient times as an herbal treatment. The leaves look suspiciously like marijuana, for those who notice such things

INTERESTING KINDS: 'Abbeville Blue' or pink 'Rosea' are to me more attractive than white 'Silver Spire'.

Loquat
Eriobotrya japonica
Sun or part shade

A handsome small tree with cut-flower quality leaves and fragrant fall flowers. The sweet spring fruit as a real plus.

FLOWER: Creamy white clusters of fragrant flowers are hidden in the foliage in the fall, with small, buttery yellow, sweet fruit with big seeds overwintering to ripen in the late winter or spring. Needs watering in some areas during dry winters for fruit to ripen well.

PLANT: Rounded multiple-branched evergreen with large oval leaves that are deeply veined and toothed.

INTERESTING KINDS: Better-fruiting named varieties include 'Gold Nugget', 'Macbeth', or late-ripening 'Thales'. Bronze loquat (*E. deflexa*) is fast growing and shrubby, easy to espalier on a fence. New leaves remain shiny bright copper for weeks; has fairly showy white spring flowers, but no fruit.

Mimosa

Albizia julibrissin

Sun

Either you like it or not, but the exotic looking "silk tree" is fast-growing and a hummingbird magnet. Very useful as a street median plant where flower and seed litter are not a problem. Its main drawback is it remains leafless longer into the spring than almost any other tree.

FLOWER: Very fragrant, fluffy, 2-inch flower balls in the summer look like airy pink pincushions. Flowers are followed by interesting flat bean pods; both are a little messy when they shed onto cars or patios.

PLANT: Small, rounded tree with a wide, nearly flat-topped canopy and ferny leaves that fold closed at night.

INTERESTING KINDS: 'Rubrum' has deep rosy-pink flowers but my favorite is 'Summer Chocolate' with nearly black-purple foliage.

Oak

Quercus species

Sun

There must be a sturdy, stately oak for every landscape setting, yet choosing the right one is crucial for happiness for both you and the tree.

FLOWER: Worm-like pollen-bearing male catkins hang from twigs in the spring, and clusters of female flowers mature into attractive fall acorns.

PLANT: Deciduous or evergreen, with leaves varying from thin and finger-like, to broad and deeply lobed. Some have fair fall colors. Water needs vary according to species.

INTERESTING KINDS: Coast live oak (*Q. agrifolia*) is a common, dependable evergreen native; Southern live oak (*Q. virginiana*) is perhaps the toughest evergreen oak in hot interior and low desert areas; cork oak (*Q. suber*) has thick bark used in making corks. Consult a dependable local nurseryman for other choices.

Olive

Olea europaea

Sun

Classic Mediterranean tree, widely grown and celebrated along streets and in gardens throughout all but the coldest mountainous parts of the state.

FLOWER: Tiny white flowers mature into olive fruit that ripens and falls (messily) late in the season and must be processed before eating. Fruitless varieties are just as attractive in the landscape.

PLANT: Gnarly old trunks and lower limbs are smooth and gray; willow-like leaves are also gray-green, which complements most other garden plants. Young trees can be pruned, thinned, and trained easily to help show off branch patterns and to reduce fruiting wood.

INTERESTING KINDS: 'Ascalona' has large fruits with small pits; 'Majestic Beauty', 'Wilsoni', and 'Swan Hill' bear little or no fruit.

Ornamental Pear

Pyrus species

Sun

In spite of small, tasteless fruit, these are popular for their outstanding spring blooms and showy fall colors. Note that only one kind flowers well along So-Cal's frost-free coast.

FLOWER: A solid mass of white apple-like blossoms appear in showy clusters just before and during spring leaf-break. Most kinds flower best after a chilly winter.

PLANT: Upright, dense, twiggy trees with a conical or spreading form. Red and burgundy fall color is usually as nice as the flower show. Plants are subject to fire blight.

INTERESTING KINDS: Only the evergreen pear (*P. kawakamii*) blooms reliably in frost-free areas. Several good ornamental pears (*P. calleryana*) are available, including pyramidal-shaped 'Redspire' (yellow to red fall color), 'Chanticleer' (orange to purple), and columnar 'Whitehouse' (reddish purple). All require considerable pruning and water, making them less tough than other selections.

Peppermint Willow
Agonis flexuosa
Sun

This somewhat generic "tree in a box" specimen, sometimes called Australian willow myrtle, is dependable as a tidy street tree and in commercial plantings where litter can be a maintenance problem. It is too often overlooked by home gardeners who need a predictable, low-maintenance shade tree for the lawn or in a large container.

FLOWER: Small white flowers are produced heavily in late spring or early summer.

PLANT: Spreading small tree with weeping branches and narrow, willow-like leaves that smell like peppermint when bruised. Trees will freeze back to the trunk in interior areas where temperatures dip into the mid-20s, but usually sprout out in the spring with no effect on summer shade.

INTERESTING KINDS: Juniper myrtle (*A. juniperina*) has fluffy white summer and fall flowers.

Pineapple Guava
Acca sellowiana
Sun or light shade

A very exotic, drought-tolerant small tree with edible exotic flowers and fruit, suitable for specimen use. Can be used as a shade tree but has messy fruit drop.

FLOWER: Very unusual inch-wide flowers of fleshy white, purple-tinged petals and frilly tufts of bright red stamens tipped with yellow pollen attract bees and hummingbirds, with less flowering in warm-winter areas. Fleshy petals are edible and can be jellied, and egg-like gray-green fruits are fragrant and sweetly acidic with tiny seeds.

PLANT: Multi-stemmed small tree with long oval leaves that are shiny green on top and silvery white underneath. Trees can be pruned or trained easily as needed, clipped as a hedge, or even espaliered.

INTERESTING KINDS: Self-fruitful varieties include 'Beechwood', 'Coolidge', 'Mammoth', 'Nazemetz', and 'Trask'.

Pines
Pinus species
Sun

Pines are absolutely not just generic green trees—every kind is distinctive, in its shape, unique needle-like leaves, bark, cones, how it responds to its growing conditions (wind, local temperatures, soil type, rainfall), and how it ages in the garden. Most can be shaped while young with selective pruning to be specimens, hedge plants, or even bonsai.

Canary Island Pine

FLOWER: Insignificant flowers. Interesting cones are highly variable, ranging from tiny round balls to huge clunkers, from smooth to spiny.

PLANT: Upright or gnarly evergreens with interesting bark textures and patterns, and needle-like leaves. Most require very well-drained or sloped soils, and are very drought tolerant once established. Note: Pines cannot be pruned hard, to where there are no needles, or the cut branches will die completely back to their point of origin. Thin entire branches or limbs, or for bushier pines cut the new-growth "candles" about halfway back in the spring.

INTERESTING KINDS: Local garden centers generally carry the best pines for your area, but several distinct kinds do well throughout most of the state. Torrey pine (*P. torreyana*) is native to coastal areas but grows well in hotter, drier areas

Torrey Pine

and in heavy soil. Also look for fast-growing calabrian pine (*P. brutia*); Canary Island pine (*P. canariensis*) with a slender trunk and tiered branches with fissured reddish bark; Mexican piñon (*P. cembroides*), a small pine with edible seeds; beach or shore pine (*P. contorta*), one of the best small pines for gardens, even in containers, but needs water; Italian stone pine (*P. pinea*) is fast growing and good for hot or beach gardens, with edible seeds.

Italian Stone Pine

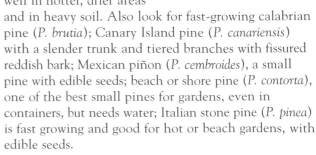

Purple-Leaf Plum
Prunus cerasifera 'Atropurpurea'
Sun

Most flowering plums produce blossoms and small fruit nearly everywhere but along So-Cal's mild-winter coastline. But this one is grown almost entirely for its gaudy purple foliage.

FLOWER: Single white flowers in spring just before and during leaf break, followed by red fruit. Rarely flowers or fruits in Southern California's mild-winter coast.

PLANT: Small rounded tree with coppery red new foliage that deepens to dark purple then red in Autumn.

INTERESTING KINDS: 'Krauter Vesuvius' has the darkest blackish-purple foliage; Catalina cherry (*P. ilicifolia lyonii*) is a native with fragrant white flowers, and pavement-staining, reddish purple edible fruit. The related Taiwan flowering cherry (*P. campanulata*) has a dependable show of purplish pink spring flowers even in warm-winter areas.

Redbud
Cercis species
Sun or light shade

Small trees with crooked limbs crusted in early spring with edible pea-like flowers (which taste exactly like raw peanuts).

FLOWER: Small blossoms clustered thickly on bare twigs and branches, followed by attractive bean pods.

PLANT: Upright with zigzag twig growth. Often short-lived. Don't prune heavily or risk losing early spring flowers.

INTERESTING KINDS: Judas tree (*C. siliquastrum*) has purplish rose flowers; flowers best with some winter chill. Mexican redbud (*C. mexicana*) has leathery blue-green leaves; Western redbud (*C. occidentalis*) is all-round attractive, from trunks and leaves to flowers and winter seedpods, plus it's drought tolerant; Eastern redbud (*C. canadensis*) cultivars including the shade-loving, purple-leaf 'Forest Pansy'.

Shoestring Acacia

Acacia stenophylla

Sun

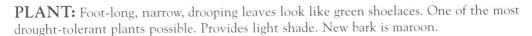

This Australian native will thrive where other trees wither away—with little or no water at all! And it tolerates reflected heat, making it an excellent tree for the edge of the street or to shade a hot afternoon wall.

FLOWER: Creamy grape-size balls in late winter and early spring.

PLANT: Foot-long, narrow, drooping leaves look like green shoelaces. One of the most drought-tolerant plants possible. Provides light shade. New bark is maroon.

INTERESTING KINDS: Many acacias are seriously invasive, especially *A. cyclops*, and are not recommended for California landscapes. However, a Southwestern desert native, *A. smallii*, while not widely available, is not invasive and has fragrant yellow spring flowers, though it might not be frost hardy; sometimes sold as *A. farnesiana*.

Silver Dollar Gum

Eucalyptus polyanthemos

Sun or light shade

Of all the many different eucalyptus (most native to Australia) which include the most widely-planted non-native species in the state, this is among the easiest and most useful as a street tree or specimen.

FLOWER: Small, non-showy whitish flowers.

PLANT: Small eucalypt with grayish juvenile leaves used in fresh and dried flower arrangements, with a distinct, pungent aroma when cut or bruised. Keep some limbs cut back to produce continual fresh stems for arrangements, because mature leaves are dark green and lance-shaped.

INTERESTING KINDS: *Eucalyptus cinerea* is a similar "silver dollar" tree used for arrangements; cider gum (*E. gunnii*) is fast growing and dense; "Black Sally" (*E. stellulata*) has unusual colored bark; coral gum (*E. torquata*) has many reddish and yellow flowers.

Smoke Tree
Cotinus coggygria
Sun or part sun

This almost unbearably exotic small tree grows best in poor soils and bad conditions. Its clouds of flowers contrast dramatically with its own foliage as well as other nearby plants.

FLOWER: Very small greenish flowers are replaced with fuzzy lavender-pink hairy stalks, in large airy masses in late summer and fall, that resemble big puffs of pink or purplish smoke.

PLANT: Bushy tree to 20 or more feet tall with oval, bluish green or more commonly burgundy or purplish leaves that usually have dramatic red, orange, or yellow fall colors.

INTERESTING KINDS: 'Royal Purple' and 'Velvet Cloak' have rich purple foliage; 'Pink Champagne' is green-leaved with pink clouds. 'Grace' is a hybrid with large deep pink puffs and purple-shaded green leaves.

Southern Magnolia
Magnolia grandiflora 'Little Gem'
Sun or moderate shade

This compact, nearly dwarf evergreen tree has fist-sized, highly-fragrant flowers over much of the summer, without being a water hog like its larger cousins.

FLOWER: Tulip-shaped white buds open into fragrant bowls of pure white with yellow stamens, followed by showy red berry-like fruits emerging from bristly pods. The longest flowering Southern magnolia.

PLANT: Upright evergreen tree has glossy deep green leaves up to 5 or 6 inches long, with fuzzy brown undersides. Leaf litter and leaf burn are less serious on this small version of the popular but ratty-looking species and larger cultivars.

INTERESTING KINDS: Stick with 'Little Gem' or plan on watering the larger kinds constantly—and still get occasional leaf drop from lack of water.

Strawberry Tree
Arbutus unedo
Sun or part shade

Very interesting as a specimen tree for a lawn or raised bed where it can be enjoyed up close, this southern European native is an attention-getter everywhere except in the coldest high mountain areas.

FLOWER: Clusters of small white or greenish urn-shaped flowers in fall and winter. Very attractive round strawberry-like fruits turn from rich golden yellow to red, and are edible though usually not tasty.

PLANT: Trunks and branches become twisted with age and have rich reddish-brown peely bark; leaves are dark green with red stems. Occasionally thin out branches to improve the shape of the tree, or plant several for a mass or hedge effect.

INTERESTING KINDS: 'Elfin King', 'Compacta', and 'Oktoberfest' are all compact, shrub-like varieties.

Sweet Bay
Laurus nobilis
Sun or light shade

The famous bay leaf used in cooking comes from this sturdy evergreen tree. Can be used as a background plant or, because it tolerates pruning very well, as a topiary, even in a large container. The plant is not fussy about anything except good drainage.

FLOWER: Clusters of small yellow flowers are followed by dark purple berries up to an inch long.

PLANT: The evergreen tree gets up to 40 feet tall, with dark green, leathery, aromatic leaves that are oval and up to 4 inches long. It suckers freely into a multi-stemmed clump, but can be thinned into a specimen or clipped into a dense hedge.

INTERESTING KINDS: 'Saratoga' is more tree-like and has broader leaves than the species.

Sweet Gum
Liquidambar styraciflua
Sun

This sidewalk-lifting tree has a real litter problem unless you choose fruitless varieties. But its toughness and intense fall colors are well worth any effort.

FLOWER: Insignificant flowers. Round, coarsely-spiked seedballs, though a sidewalk or lawn nuisance, are very attractive on the tree in winter.

PLANT: Fast-growing tree with pointy star-shaped leaves with brilliant fall colors of yellow, red, maroon, and purple, even in mild-winter areas. Branches have furrowed bark and corky lengthwise "wings" for winter interest and use in floral arrangements. Resists oak root rot.

INTERESTING KINDS: California-bred 'Burgundy', 'Festival', and 'Palo Alto' have great fall colors. 'Variegata' has yellow blotches on the leaves. 'Rotundiloba' (pictured) has smoothly-rounded rather than pointed leaf lobes, plus little or no seedpods (neither does 'Cherokee'). Chinese sweetgum (*L. formosana*) has fewer root problems than the others.

Bald Cypress

Other Good Trees:

Bald Cypress (*Taxodium distichum*) is a fast-growing, ferny-leaved tree that quickly outgrows "garden size" landscapes and is hard to grow other plants underneath. Montezuma cypress (*T. mucronatum*) is slower growing and more graceful, but hard to find commercially.

Blue Elderberry (*Sambucus mexicana*) is a California native with divided leaves and large, flat-topped clusters of white spring and summer flowers followed by blue-black berries used in jellies, pies, and wine.

Camphor Tree (*Cinnamomum camphora*) has sturdy limbs, colorful and aromatic foliage (new growth is reddish or bronze before turning to shiny yellow green) and fragrant yellow flowers, but can get root rot in heavy or wet soils.

Carolina Cherry Laurel (*Prunus caroliniana*) is a fast-growing evergreen with dense branches and dark glossy foliage, plus fragrant small white spring flowers; resents reflected heat and needs water in dry areas.

Catalina Ironwood (*Lyonothamnus floribundus* ssp. *aspleniifolius*) is a striking native tree with long, deeply divided (marijuana-like) leaves, flat clusters of early summer flowers, and very attractive peeling reddish bark. Requires good drainage; grows best near the coast.

Japanese Pagoda (*Sophora japonica*) has showy, droopy clusters of yellowish white summer flowers and interesting constricted, beaded necklace-like seed-pods; grows poorly in cool damp climates.

Knobcone Pine (*Pinus attenuata*) is a fast-growing pine for hot areas and poor soil, but grows poorly near the coast.

Carolina Cherry Laurel

Lacebark Elm (*Ulmus parvifolia*) is a highly prized small shade, patio, or street tree with beautifully mottled bark, but its invasive roots make it a greedy thug, plus its weak limbs break easily in storms. Sorry!

Redwood (*Sequoia sempervirens*), a signature California native, grows very quickly but resents reflected heat and requires regular watering and iron nutrients to remain nice and green.

Soapberry (*Sapindus drummondii*) is similar to golden rain tree (*Koelreuteria*) but nearly impossible to find commercially and fairly weedy with seedlings.

Sour Gum (*Nyssa sylvatica*) has outstanding red fall color even in mild-winter areas, but needs a deep well-drained soil and does not tolerate polluted air.

Sycamore (*Platanus* species, including California sycamore, *P. racemosa*) is big and has a serious leaf litter problem as a street tree or in small gardens, and is seriously disease prone.

Soapberry

AN INSTANT "TREE" IS EASIER THAN YOU'D THINK—if you think about how easy a large deck umbrella can be. One large-diameter post, at least 10 feet high, set into the ground then planted with a vine, can create the same effect as a small tree. Setting up a two-post arbor—again, at least 10 feet high, using 6-by-6-foot posts instead of cheap 4-by-4's—is only a little more expensive, with nearly twice the appeal. See the vines chapter for more ideas.

Texas Mountain Laurel (*Sophora secundiflora*) has sweetly scented, wisteria-like, violet-blue winter and early spring flowers; very interesting seedpods but seeds are poisonous. Hard to find.

Toyon (*Heteromeles arbutifolia*) is a good, tough native for informal landscapes or where it can be pruned judiciously to leave year-old wood on which summer flowers and red berries are produced.

Wax Myrtle (*Myrica californica*) is an outstanding native shrub or small tree with aromatic foliage and purplish, waxy, berry-like nutlets, but it is untidy except in naturalistic gardens and needs frequent pruning.

Texas Mountain Laurel

 Best for Beginners:

- *Chinese Pistache*
- *Crape Myrtle*
- *Eucalyptus*
- *Ginkgo*

- *Japanese Persimmon*
- *Loquat*
- *Oaks*

- *Olive*
- *Purple-Leaf Plum*
- *Red Maple*

Kinda Tricky:

- *Citrus* (most types)
- *Fig* (gophers)
- *Magnolia* (water hog)

- *Mimosa* (litter problems)

- *Sweetgum* (litter problems)

California Urban State Tree

Okay, okay, so the official California state tree is the redwood (*Sequoia sempervirens*)—though there are some folks who think the Joshua tree is more appropriate for desert areas. There are other unique trees found all over the state (none more stunning than a blue ball tree in an art park just outside Sonoma [see page 10]).

But in the past couple of decades, invasive exotic "cell tower trees" have become widespread even in rural areas, where they are tolerated as necessary evils. In an attempt to fit into sensitive areas (some say by the hand of an intelligent designer), a few have adapted themselves to local landscapes.

I suggest that we recognize the following now-common creatures as the official "urban tree" because it symbolizes the progressive nature of citizens of the great state of California.

Cell Tower Tree
Communicanna species
Sun

FLOWER: None, though sometimes large bird nests can be found among the foliage.

PLANT: Narrow, erect single trunk, never branching, to 40 or more feet tall, topped with dark, stiff, outward-radiating foliage. Needs no care other than occasional upgrades or wiring done by professionals.

INTERESTING KINDS: Pine-leaf (*C. pinus*) is the most widely used cultivar, though palm-leaf (*C. cretaceous*) can be found near upscale neighborhoods. The ubiquitous freeway species (*C. vulgaris*) is so common as to almost be unnoticeable. A rare variegated form (*C. vulgaris* 'Camouflage') has been spotted in natural areas.

Vines
WITH VIGOR

Climbing vines are the most overlooked group of plants available to gardeners. Yet they are everywhere, clambering up trees in the native woods, sprawling along roadsides, cascading down hillsides and creek banks, and softening the edges of fences and arbors in every small town and country garden. Look around—there are dozens of great vines that need little or no care at all, other than occasional pruning to keep them out of our faces and off of other plants.

Technically, vines are just flexible stems that don't stop growing; they constantly get longer, reach higher, and spread into new areas. Some are multiple-branched and make good screens or ground-covers. There are annuals to be replanted every year or tender tropical plants that must be brought in during winter. Others are herbaceous perennials that leap from the ground each spring or long-lived woody landscape features that provide a year-round framework of texture for many years. Some grow so fast they can take over a porch in a few weeks; others seem to take forever to get established and depend on their supports to give the desired vertical effect until they catch on.

Vines and their supports lend crucial "vertical appeal" to

Red Leaf Grape Vine

landscapes. They provide framing, create focal points, and lift our view from the lawn and flower beds to eye level and above. They mask bare walls to provide fast shade on the hot side of a house or hide ugly scenery. Several provide erosion control or grow in areas that are too difficult to mow or too shady for grass. They provide colorful flowers in the spring, summer, and fall; gorgeous autumn colors; and evergreen texture or accents through our seasonal "down times." On the following pages are a few easy vines for California.

Clock Vine

BOTANICAL PYTHONS SUCH AS HONEYSUCKLE are normally not the first—or even the last—choices for use in landscapes, but they can have their places. Some gardeners and naturalists get upset over the use of "invasive exotic" plants in landscapes because they have escaped from gardens and begun to take over natural areas, sometimes displacing native plants, and are difficult or expensive to control. Just as rampant native vines can be carefully placed and tended, most invasive non-natives can be controlled or converted into mannerly garden favorites.

But it is important to consider the impact of aggressive vines on neighbors and nearby natural areas. Think twice or more before planting them, make sure they are in a good spot for control, and take care to keep them in bounds. When selecting overly vigorous vines, consider how far they can reach. Place them away from other plants and make sure you can at least walk all the way around them, keep an eye on errant shoots, and prune or mow what is not wanted. If you choose to grow weedy vines, even with great care, expect criticism—but hold up your head and go on. After all, every plant is a weed somewhere.

DON'T BE WEAK WHEN IT COMES TO MAKING AN ARBOR, PERGOLA, OR OTHER VINE SUPPORT. Vines often outgrow flimsy "store-bought" arbors, and it isn't unusual for climbing roses and wisteria to tear up wooden lattice. Use sturdy 4-by-6 or 6-by-6-foot posts at least 10 feet high to allow for vines to grow over and hang down a bit. One of the best "fabrics" for use between heavy posts is heavy-gauge concrete reinforcing mesh, with large openings to allow vines to grow through readily.

Annual Vines

Some vines have to be replanted every year—some are perennials in other areas but can't make it for one reason or another in yours, others are just too much trouble to keep alive and are very easy to grow from seed. Any good garden book will have detailed instructions on sprouting seed and creating different kinds of support. A few easy, popular kinds from seed are sweet pea, scarlet runner bean, nasturtium, moonflower, hyacinth bean, gourds, cypress vine, and black-eyed Susan vine.

 **Best for Beginners:**

- *Boston Ivy*
- *Bougainvillea*
- *Climbing Roses*
- *Coral Vine*
- *Creeping Fig*
- *Fatshedera*
- *Star Jasmine*
- *Virginia Creeper*

Kinda Tricky:

- *Grape*
- *Jasmine*
- *Passion Vine* (rampant)
- *Wisteria* (needs lots of pruning and training)

Black-Eyed Susan Vine
Thunbergia alata
Sun

Because it grows and flowers so quickly from seed, this So-Cal perennial vine is usually treated as an annual, especially in containers or hanging baskets.

FLOWER: Short tubular flowers flare out to an inch wide and are produced freely as long as the weather is warm. Spent flowers shed neatly, leaving a clean vine and colorful carpet underneath the plant.

PLANT: Triangular green leaves on a fast-growing, twining vine. Seed can be started indoors and transplanted any time the soil is warm. Also grows and flowers well in greenhouses, or indoors where sun is bright and humidity is high.

INTERESTING KINDS: Yellow, orange or white selections are available. Orange clock vine (*T. gregorii*) has gray-green leaves and bright orange flowers all season.

Boston Ivy
Parthenocissus tricuspidata
Sun or part shade

The ivy of Ivy League colleges is one of the most vigorous vines, covering entire walls in one or two seasons, and has among the most dependable fall color shows of all.

FLOWER: Not significant; neither is the fruit.

PLANT: Fast-climbing, clinging tightly to surfaces with suction disks at ends of tendrils, naturally branches to make a dense mat of foliage. Generally three-lobed leaves are glossy and up to 8 inches wide, and turn orange to deep red in fall. In hot areas avoid hot places—plant on northern or eastern walls, not west or south.

INTERESTING KINDS: 'Green Showers' has larger leaves that turn burgundy in the fall. 'Lowii' and 'Veitchii' have smaller leaves and are good for smaller spaces since they are less vigorous.

Bougainvillea
Bougainvillea hybrids
Sun

This heat-loving tropical, planted almost to excess even where frosts damage or kill those planted in the ground, has the most punched-up vibrant colors in the state. Fast and easy container-grown replacements are always available.

FLOWER: Clusters of colorful papery bracts surround small tube-like real flowers from spring to fall or even into winter in warm areas. Requires neglect to bloom well.

PLANT: Fast growing with medium green or variegated leaves. Needs to be tied to a sturdy support or it can ramble in and around chain link fences; can be pruned and trained as a small shrub or specimen plant, or allowed to cascade from containers or walls.

INTERESTING KINDS: Among the hardiest are 'San Diego Red', 'Hawaii', 'Lavender Queen', and 'Barbara Karst'.

Carolina Jessamine
Gelsemium sempervirens
Sun or part shade

One of the first vines to bloom in late winter, the native jessamine twists its way to the tops of trees and shrubs. It's a favorite vine for small arbors where evergreen screening is needed, but can tear up latticework. Prune after flowering to keep it in bounds.

FLOWER: Cheerful, medium-yellow trumpets up to 2 inches long are produced in great clusters in the late winter, with an occasional flush of flowers in the summer and fall.

PLANT: Moderate grower to 20 or more feet, many stems wrapping and twisting around supports. Can be a loose groundcover, especially on banks. The small, pointed leaves are evergreen.

INTERESTING KINDS: 'Lemon Drop' is very fragrant; 'Butterscotch' flowers again in the fall; 'Pride of Augusta' is double-flowering; all may be hard to find locally.

Cat's Claw
Macfadyena unguis-cati
Sun or part shade

The long-lived "yellow trumpet vine" climbs fast and high, and thrives in the hottest conditions, making it a good vine for south or west walls to reduce summer heat gain for homes. It can be used to screen old buildings and will outlast trees it climbs.

FLOWER: Spring masses of bright yellow trumpets 3 or 4 inches across, followed by foot or more long, thin but flattened bean-like seedpods that remain on the vine for months.

PLANT: Interesting paired leaflets with frilly tendrils that use "claws" to hook onto nearly anything—even concrete walls! Stems also root as they grow and attach to wood or other porous surfaces. Evergreen in mild winter areas, deciduous during heaviest frosts.

INTERESTING KINDS: Only the species is available.

Climbing Hydrangea
Hydrangea anomala ssp. petiolaris
Part sun or light shade

Though without support this plant is naturally a sprawling shrub, it is very vigorous when trained or pegged to climb against walls. The long-lived vine can easily get to 40 or 50 feet or more high or wide, with very showy blooms and long-lasting flowers.

FLOWER: Late spring or early summer, short flowering stems produce many flat, lace-cap- type white flowers 8 to 10 inches across. Thin some of the branches or flowering stems to get bigger flowers.

PLANT: Heart-shaped leaves are deep green until shedding in the fall. The vine is slow to get established, but eventually needs thinning to shape or train the plant.

INTERESTING KINDS: The species is showy and most commonly available.

'New Dawn'

Climbing Roses
Rosa species and hybrids
Sun

There are quite a few disease-free climbing roses to cover arches, walls, and fences with beauty and scent, without a lot of trouble.

FLOWER: Loose clusters of often-fragrant pink, white, red, or yellow flowers. Some types have showy fruits.

PLANT: Vining shrubs that need to be tied to supports, with usually thorny canes reaching several yards long. Prune any time to remove older or wayward canes.

- **Lady Banks' Rose** (*R. banksiae* and variety 'Lutea'), thornless vine with dusty yellow or fragrant white flowers in the spring only.
- **Cherokee Rose** (*R. laevigata*), once-bloomer with huge white flowers.
- **'Climbing Cécile Brünner'**, dependable medium pink.
- **'New Dawn'**, prolific with huge pinkish-white fragrant flowers.
- **'Don Juan'**, hearty red climber.
- **'Zéphirine Drouhin'**, thornless and dark pink.
- **'Red Cascades'**, small nonstop red rambler.
- **'Climbing Iceberg'**, white.
- **'Golden Showers'**, yellow.

TIP ON PRUNING CLIMBING ROSES: Thin cluttered stems in the winter when you can see what you are doing better. Through the growing season snip off wayward canes as needed, cutting back to just above a leaf or leaf bud pointing the direction you want new growth to go.

Lady Banks' Rose

Coral Vine

Antigonon leptopus

Sun or part sun

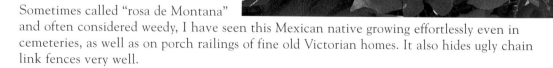

Sometimes called "rosa de Montana" and often considered weedy, I have seen this Mexican native growing effortlessly even in cemeteries, as well as on porch railings of fine old Victorian homes. It also hides ugly chain link fences very well.

FLOWER: Lacy, arching sprays of coral pink flowers are produced continuously to create an incredibly airy effect

PLANT: Twining, lightly branching vine sprouts from an underground tuber and can climb 20 feet or more with bright green, arrowhead shaped leaves up to 5 inches long. A cold winter will kill it back to the ground, but it returns quickly in the spring. Grows readily from seeds.

INTERESTING KINDS: 'Alba' has white flowers; 'Baja Red' is deep pink; 'Rubrum' is nearly red.

Creeping Fig

Ficus pumila

Sun or part shade

One of California's mainstay evergreens for covering brick garden and house walls, or even on the facings or risers of garden steps, this true member of the fig family grows close against any support it bumps into.

FLOWER: Small oblong "fruits" which are really closed flowers. Not showy.

PLANT: The slow-growing, semi-branching vine is covered with small, heart-shaped leaves that can get up to 4 inches long and half as wide on mature plants. It can cover a two- or three-story structure, climbing with clinging roots that can literally take the paint off a wall. It has the milky sap of a true fig.

INTERESTING KINDS: 'Minima' remains small and compact; 'Variegata' has creamy yellow markings.

Cross Vine

Bignonia capreolata

Sun or part shade

The thumb-size flowers of this high-climbing native vine are very attractive to hummingbirds. Rapid growth makes the vine ideal for covering walls.

FLOWER: Fat orange buds open into 2-inch trumpets with two lips, reddish orange on the outside and yellowish on the inside, produced in loose clusters in leaf joints.

PLANT: Fast-growing to 50 feet or more, usually flowering only where it finds sunlight. Oblong leaves are 4 inches long, with a pair of leaflets on both sides of the leaf joints like four large butterfly wings. Grows by twining and clasping with strong tendrils that wrap or stick tightly to whatever surface they touch.

INTERESTING KINDS: Free-blooming 'Tangerine Beauty' has exceptionally bright, apricot-orange tubes; 'Shalimar Red' repeat blooms with reddish flowers and yellow throats.

Cypress Vine

Ipomoea quamoclit

Sun or very light shade

This delicate, ferny vine is so easy you might actually regret getting it started. The incredibly fast-growing annual vine can wrap up everything within reach. Pull up excess in the summer, and leave just enough to enjoy.

FLOWER: Bright red, flaring tubular darlings scattered profusely over the entire vine, right up until frost. One of the best butterfly and hummingbird flowers around, yet too small to be as attractive to heavy bees. Note: Some coastal areas are not hot enough for outstanding flower production.

PLANT: Super-fast-growing twining vine, thick enough to make a light groundcover. Foliage is airy and ferny. Vine can overpower nearby small shrubs and escape by seed.

INTERESTING KINDS: Only the species is widely available.

Fatshedera
× *Fatshedera lizei*
Part shade or shade

This unusual but durable hybrid between the large-leaf shrub *Fatsia japonica* and its rambling close relative English ivy (*Hedera helix*), got the best of both parents—a floppy, big-leaf "ivy on steroids" that doesn't become invasive.

FLOWER: Umbel-like panicles of sterile white flowers.

PLANT: Semi-erect, slow-growing, branching vine with wide, ivy-like leaves up to 10 inches across with three to five pointed tips. Can be staked or tied like a short vine, or pinched to make it a small bush.

INTERESTING KINDS: 'Variegata' has leaves bordered with white; each leaf of 'Media-Picta' has a central yellow botch. New 'Aurea Maculata' has glossy leaves up to 10 inches wide on red stems, with light green and white splotches in the center of each.

Gourds
Lagenaria, Luffa, or *Cucurbita*
Sun

A friend once called gourds "vegetal white-out" for their ability to cover stuff up. Rampant growers are festooned with large ornamental fruits.

FLOWER: Loofah and small kinds of gourds have small, yellow flowers; large true gourds have big, flat, white flowers. Separate male and female flowers are produced on the same plants.

PLANT: Fast-growing vines with large leaves that climb 15 feet or more, using strong, long tendrils to wrap around everything they touch. The lush growth of the gourd vine can shade out other plants.

INTERESTING KINDS: Loofah can be skinned and the insides used like a sponge, dishrag, or bath scrubber. Also try long-handled dipper, bird house, and small ornamental gourds in many shapes, sizes, and colors.

Grape
Vitis species
Sun

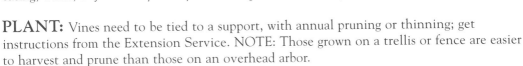

Forget the berries; these vines are exceptional ornamentals all year—covering an arbor in a season, with bold foliage and attractive trunk and canes in the winter as well. Berries are a useful bonus.

FLOWER: Small non-showy clusters. Juicy berries used for fresh eating, wines, or jellies vary widely between species and variety.

PLANT: Vines need to be tied to a support, with annual pruning or thinning; get instructions from the Extension Service. NOTE: Those grown on a trellis or fence are easier to harvest and prune than those on an overhead arbor.

INTERESTING KINDS: The native *Vitis californica* has tiny fruit, but is highly ornamental with spectacular red, orange, and purple fall foliage—and needs no water. 'Roger's Red', 'Russian River', 'Walker Ridge' are good fall-color selections.

Hyacinth Bean
Lablab purpureus
Sun

This is one traffic-stopping vine, with its attractive foliage, flowers, and beans. Easy to grow on small arbors, but never a weedy nuisance, this historic vine (grown by Thomas Jefferson) is as easy as can be, and fast growing from seed to flower.

FLOWER: Upright spikes of very attractive lavender-purple, sweet pea-like flowers stand above the foliage, followed by flat, dark, burgundy-purple bean pods 3 inches or so long. Seeds are black with a white edge.

PLANT: Twining summer annual vine with large, divided green leaves can easily reach the top of an arbor, but rarely ventures beyond.

INTERESTING KINDS: 'Purple Darkness' has purple-green foliage and lavender and white flowers.

Jasmine or Poet's Jasmine

Jasminum officinale
Sun or light shade

Not all jasmines are created equal—some of the most popular need a long, hot growing season to flower well, and are frost-sensitive. The poet's jasmine is dependably vigorous and long flowering throughout most of the state.

FLOWER: White flowers up to an inch across are produced in clusters from spring into fall. One of the most fragrant hardy vines.

PLANT: Semi-evergreen vine with rich green summer leaves, each with multiple leaflets.

INTERESTING KINDS: Spanish jasmine (*J. officinale affine*) is a smaller, tidier form with larger (1¹/₂ inch) flowers. Both Italian jasmine (*J. humile*) and primrose jasmine (*J. mesnyi*) are evergreen vining shrubs (can be trained either as a vine or shrub) with yellow flowers.

Mandevilla

Mandevilla splendens
Sun or part shade

A short but sexy vine with big leaves and huge pink flowers, this tender tropical is easiest to handle when grown in a pot near a small arbor, or with its own arbor frame in the pot.

FLOWER: Flared trumpets in several shades of pink or white are 3 to 5 inches wide, blooming spring, summer, and fall. Easy to get to flower, even when starting with a small potted plant.

PLANT: Twining vine to 20 feet long, usually pinched to keep it shorter and bushier.

INTERESTING KINDS: *Mandevilla* × *amabilis* 'Alice du Pont' is a very common and popular hybrid, but 'Ruby Star' is more compact.

Moonflower or Moonvine

Ipomoea alba

Sun or very light shade

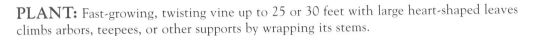

One of the most magical events in a new gardener's life is watching moonflowers open at dusk. The large white flowers spring suddenly from relatively small "twists" of buds, releasing a fragrance into the evening air that all but overwhelms anyone whose nose is too close. Large night-flying moths are interesting pollinators.

FLOWER: Flat white fragrant trumpets, up to 6 inches across, open in the evening from pointed buds shaped like swirls of soft ice cream. Very fragrant, and almost glow in the dark.

PLANT: Fast-growing, twisting vine up to 25 or 30 feet with large heart-shaped leaves climbs arbors, teepees, or other supports by wrapping its stems.

INTERESTING KINDS: Only the species is available. Morning glory, sweet potato vine, and cypress vine are relatives.

Nasturtium

Tropaeolum majus

Sun or light shade

This old-fashioned favorite plant has "taken over" garden fences, then kept going into neighbors' gardens, then on along highway ditches and into nearby canyons. Foliage is distinctive, and cutting-quality flowers are edible.

FLOWER: Flaring, long-spurred blooms up to $2^1/_2$ inches across come in maroon, red, orange, yellow, and creamy white. Along with flowers, young leaves and seedpods can be eaten raw.

PLANT: Rapidly-growing climbing kinds of nasturtium clamber over any support by coiling leaf stalks. Rounded leaves on long stems are green or variegated. In mild-winter/hot summer areas sow seed in the fall for winter and spring blooms.

INTERESTING KINDS: Various good strains include both single- and double-flowering forms, in single colors or mixed. Bush forms are also widely available.

Passion Vine
Passiflora species
Sun

These aggressive vines can be real thugs, spreading in even extremely poor soils, climbing and wrapping over everything they get close to. But the spicy-scented flowers are among the most exotic looking in the garden.

FLOWER: Complex frilly disks of purple, blue, lavender, red, or white are produced non-stop, followed by oblong fleshy fruits.

PLANT: Rapidly growing stems that twine and wrap with tendrils, to 20, 30 or more feet in a season; can spread by suckers. This tough plant is not considered low maintenance because of routine invasion control pruning. One of the Gulf fritillary butterfly's main host plants—just deal with the caterpillar damage, okay? The plant will recover and re-leaf, even if completely denuded.

INTERESTING KINDS: Many are available, all interesting, but ask around before planting—some can become a beautiful nightmare!

Potato Vine
Solanum jasminoides
Sun or light shade

If it's a fast-growing vine and non-stop flowering you need, this one will do the trick—and then some. This potato and eggplant relative also provides dependable light shade on arbors without being too messy.

FLOWER: White, star-shaped flowers with yellow stamens that form a little pointed "teepee" in the center, are about an inch wide, arranged in loose, hanging clusters, blooming most heavily in spring though with a moderate show in the fall.

PLANT: Fast-growing twining vine is evergreen or nearly so, with arrow-shaped leaves up to 3 inches long tinged slightly with purple. Makes a good shade vine for arbors or trellises. Prune heavily occasionally to reduce clutter, and cut rambling runners as needed.

INTERESTING KINDS: 'Variegatum' has white markings on the leaves.

Scarlet Runner Bean
Phaseolus coccineus
Sun

Love having plants that are pretty, but that you can eat as well? This heirloom bean makes a handsome tee-pee plant, or can be grown to provide shade on an arbor or beside a porch.

FLOWER: Slender clusters of vivid scarlet and white flowers are produced continually through the growing season, followed by very dark, flat bean pods. Young beans are edible, but get very tough as they mature; older beans can be shelled and eaten like limas.

PLANT: Twisting perennial vine is frost sensitive and grown entirely as an annual.

INTERESTING KINDS: Pink and white varieties are available from mail-order sources. Other interesting beans can be grown as ornamentals, including snap beans with purple pods (which change to green when cooked).

Scarlet Trumpet Vine
Distictis buccinatoria
Sun

A Mexican native with dense foliage and a spectacular flower show during the heat of summer, and during every warm spell that comes along.

FLOWER: Blood-red to orange-red flared trumpet flowers with bright yellow throats, up to 4 inches long, stand out in clusters from the vine during warm periods, followed by pods of flattened seeds

PLANT: Evergreen vines, with glossy leaves that each have two oblong or oval leaflets and a three-forked tendril with suction-cup appendages that the plant uses to climb. May temporarily defoliate during drought, high winds, or cold temperatures. Plant in a protected place in interior areas where freezes are likely.

INTERESTING KINDS: This is the most cold hardy of the *Distictis* genus.

Star Jasmine or Confederate Jasmine

Trachelospermum jasminoides

Sun or light shade

One of the most popular old fragrant vines, almost supports itself and its glossy leaves and fragrant flowers, even on an arbor in the shade. Also makes a superb groundcover for sun or shade—a non-invasive ivy substitute.

FLOWER: The display and delicious fragrance of snow-white, pinwheel-shaped blossoms begins heavily in the spring, and continues for several weeks into early summer. Good for bees, so don't plant by a door.

PLANT: Dense vine with very glossy, 2- to 3-inch leaves climbs by twining to 20 or more feet with even longer shoots but can be kept pruned onto a wall or smaller trellis, or kept on a mailbox or used as a dense groundcover.

INTERESTING KINDS: 'Variegatum' has creamy yellow blotches on deep green leaves.

Sweet Pea

Lathyrus odoratus

Sun or light shade

Perhaps the most nostalgic vine from grandmother's garden, these showy, fragrant flowers love warm days and cool nights.

FLOWER: Very showy, usually sweetly-fragrant pea-like flowers in masses of rose, blue, purple, pink, white, scarlet, salmon, and mixed or bicolors. Selections can be found to bloom in winter, but spring- and summer-flowering kinds are "day-length sensitive" and won't bloom until days are at least fourteen or fifteen hours long. Excellent as cut flowers.

PLANT: Small vine to 4 or 5 feet or so, climbs with tendrils. Soak seed before planting to hasten germination.

INTERESTING KINDS: Too many to single out. Try a mix of modern hybrids and heirlooms, all readily available from seed racks or mail order.

Trumpet Vine
Campsis × tagliabuana
Sun or light shade

This vigorous, long-lived hybrid between scarlet trumpet vine (*C. radicans*) and a Chinese species gives fast coverage and attracts hummingbirds. Plant where you can walk around it for maintenance or it will take over!

FLOWER: Summer clusters of thumb-sized trumpets of bright orange, red, or salmon, followed by large, canoe-like seedpods 5 to 6 inches long.

PLANT: Extremely vigorous vine climbs 40 or more feet long by twisting and attaching with aerial roots—even onto metal poles, plus it spreads by underground suckers. Foot-long leaves hold nine or more pointed leaflets.

INTERESTING KINDS: 'Madame Galen' has bright orange-red flowers; 'Crimson Trumpet' is deep red. Chinese trumpet vine (*C. grandiflora*) is not as large but has slightly larger, red flowers; 'Morning Charm' has peach-colored flowers.

Violet Trumpet Vine
Clytostoma callistegioides
Sun or light shade

This durable, very drought-tolerant vine uses tendrils to clamber quickly over everything in its path, needing a fence or other large space for elbowroom.

FLOWER: Three-inch-long trumpets of violet, lavender, or pale purple appear on the tips and new stems from late spring to fall.

PLANT: Strong vine with leaves divided into two glossy green leaflets that have wavy margins. New shoots at the ends hang downward in a curtain of leaves and flowers. Keep in bounds by pruning in the late winter and removing long runners trying to get out of control.

INTERESTING KINDS: Only the species is available

Virginia Creeper
Parthenocissus quinquefolia
Sun or light shade

This very vigorous relative of Boston ivy clambers over everything in its path then cascades back down to start over again. Fabulous fall colors on plants grown in full sun and never watered.

FLOWER: Not noticeable, but very attractive blue-black berries in the fall are held by bright red stems.

PLANT: Fast-growing, native climbing vine or spreading groundcover has hand-like leaves of five long, toothed leaflets, bronzy at first then turning glossy green, and with brilliant burgundy red fall colors. Attaches with suction-like disks on short tendrils; can get under shingles or into window frames.

INTERESTING KINDS: *Parthenocissus henryana*, the silvervein creeper, is a refined version of Virginia creeper, with black-green leaves embroidered with silver veins and flushed with red-purple beneath.

Wisteria
Wisteria species
Sun

Beautiful and fragrant wisteria is an almost overwhelmingly huge plant, but great for arbors.

FLOWER: Unsurpassable chains of deliciously fragrant purple, white, or pink flowers right before and during spring. Flowers best in low-fertility soil, or risk having all vine and no flowers. Velvety seedpods hang on long after leaves shed in the fall.

PLANT: Twining vine without tendrils with long leaves divided into many smaller leaflets, can spread quickly by runners, or can be pruned into a freestanding specimen.

INTERESTING KINDS: Japanese wisteria (*W. floribunda*) has long flower chains; silky wisteria (*W. venusta*), both the white and purple, has the biggest flowers on the longest stalks. Chinese wisteria (*W. sinensis*) can bloom twice a year, following hard pruning right after spring flowers begin to fade.

Other Good Vines:

Bower Vine, Wonga Wonga (*Pandorea pandorana*) is exceptionally beautiful in or out of bloom, but is not completely hardy in hot inland gardens.

Burmese Honeysuckle (*Lonicera hildebrandiana*) is an oversized vine with large leaves and huge honeysuckle flowers. Will not tolerate a freeze.

Chalice Vine or **Gold Cup Vine** (*Solandra maxima*) has fantastic golden-yellow flowers like large wine cups, but is limited to the warm southern areas of California.

Coral Honeysuckle (*Lonicera sempervirens*), native to more humid Eastern states, is a semi-evergreen small vine with clusters of orange-red narrow tubes, good for hummingbirds.

Chilean Jasmine (*Mandevilla laxa*) has heart-shaped leaves and white flowers with a gardenia-like perfume. Hardier and requires less heat to bloom than the larger, showier hybrid mandevillas.

Lilac Vine (*Hardenbergia violacea*) is a medium-size vine with lots of sweet pea-like flowers in long clusters. Includes pinkish purple 'Happy Wanderer', white 'Icicle', and pink *H. violacea* var. *rosea*.

Mexican Flame Vine (*Senecio confusus*), perennial in warm areas, has clusters of bright reddish-orange with golden centers, very showy and a butterfly magnet. 'Sao Paulo' has deep orange flowers.

Pelican Flower (*Aristolochia grandiflora*) is—how can I put it?—*awesome*, with its thick mass of shingles of leaves and bizarre monstrosity flowers, a foot or more long with a weird pouch and appendages. In cool-climate areas grow it on a warm wall, or in a container to save over winter.

Bougainvillea

Tacky or Gaudy

As if Hawaiian ti plants, bougain-villea vines, and red convertibles aren't gaudy enough, gardeners in the Golden State seem overly indulgent of kitsch.

Not that kitsch is entirely bad. Generally thought of condescendingly as relating to "low brow" taste, it can also represent a sense of irony ("this stuff is so bad, it's good"). More than simply art gone wrong, it allows ordinary people to participate in romantic fantasy, or poke fun at the sometimes-bittersweet blandness of life.

Besides, there is a tacit differ-ence between "tacky" and "gaudy." Gaudy is when you do something that others may not like, but they cut you some slack if they think you know what you're doing. Tacky, on

the other hand, is when you just don't know any better—bless your heart! But filmmaker John Waters even defined the difference between good and bad tacky, "Good tacky looks up to its subject; bad tacky looks down."

Take plastic pink flamingos—America's most loved-to-be-hated icon, patented in 1957 by Massachusetts art school graduate Donald Featherstone. His company churns out over 250,000 pairs of flamingos a year—and not all go into yards of the terminally tacky. "I don't think it's always a joke," Featherstone said. "The majority of the people who buy them just really feel that an empty yard, like an empty coffee table, cries out for something. They don't do it for themselves, but to entertain you.

"We actually sell more plastic ducks than flamingos, but I gotta say, the duck people aren't like flamingo people. Folks who put out flamingos are friendlier than others."

So if you have a hankering to put out a giant seashell, old boat, mini-lighthouse, concrete seahorse, cutout mermaids, nylon hibiscus flag, fake pirate cannon, themed party lights, or a cute mailbox made to look like a whale, dolphin, mermaid, sea turtle, fish, pelican, or surfboard, keep in mind what Featherstone once told me: "Before plastic, only the wealthy could afford to have poor taste."

Index

Meet the Author

Felder Rushing, who attended kindergarten in the Mojave Desert's China Lake, is a tenth-generation American gardener whose quirky, overstuffed cottage garden has been featured in many magazines, including *Garden Design, Landscape Architecture, House and Garden, The New York Times, Organic Gardening,* and *Better Homes and Gardens.* He holds two horticulture degrees and works closely with botanic gardens and university horticulturists coast to coast, often conducting advanced Master Gardener training.

During the 1970's, while touring the West Coast from Hotel del Coronado to county fairs as a mediocre musician, he installed irrigation and landscapes for a San Diego garden center. He has studied plants at Huntington Botanical Garden, U.C. Davis Arboretum, Quail Botanical Garden, Berkeley Botanical Garden, *Sunset Magazine* demonstration garden, Garden of the Sun in Fresno, Golden Gate Botanical Garden, Santa Monica Botanical Garden, Hearst Castle gardens, Filoli, Santa Barbara Botanical Garden, Lotusland, and many old Mission gardens. And he has explored thousands of others, both public and private, across North, Central, and South America, Europe, Africa, and the Caribbean.

Rushing has presented over a hundred lectures a year, coast to coast, ifor the Southern California Horticulture Society in Los Angeles, the San Diego Horticulture Society, the Quail Botanical Garden in Encinitas, the Master Gardener conference at Asilomar State Park in Carmel, the Monterrey Flower Show, the Fresno Garden Show, and the Copia Center in Napa.

Felder has been an active (though distinctly unstuffy) member of over a dozen plant societies. He is on the board of directors of the American Horticultural Society, and has been a national director of the Garden Writers Association.

Felder's fourteen garden books include the award-winning *Passalong Plants,* named the "best written" garden book in the country by the Garden Writers Association. He writes a syndicated newspaper gardening column, hosts a live garden program on National Public Radio affiliates, and has appeared on HGTV, Educational TV, and the Discovery Channel. Hundreds of his articles and photographs have appeared in such magazines as *National Geographic, Fine Gardening, Organic Gardening, National Wildflower Journal, Country Living Gardener,* and many others. He has served as a contributing editor for Garden Design and Horticulture magazines.

Believing that too many of his fellow horticulturists complicate things unnecessarily, Felder says "We are daunted, not dumb." He has spent a lifetime trying to make gardening as easy as it is fun.

Felder with one of his brothers,
Mojave Desert, 1954.

LP 707   172